Contents

FOCUS ON JOHN

a study guide for
groups & individuals

revised edition

by
Dr. Stanley H. Purdam
&
Kathleen Mulhern

Formerly published as *Focus on the Gospel of John*.

Living the Good News
   a division of The Morehouse Group
Editorial Offices
600 Grant, Suite 400
Denver, CO 80203

Cover and interior design: Polly Christensen

ISBN 1-889108-66-9

Introduction to the Focus Series

THE FOCUS BIBLE STUDY SERIES offers a unique and inviting way to interact with and experience God's word, allowing that word to filter into every area of life. They are designed to challenge growing Christians to explore scripture and expand their understanding of God's call. The studies echo the **Living the Good News** strategy of experiential learning; that is, they welcome the participant into a journey of discovery.

Journal Format

Focus Bible Studies are adaptable for individual use or group use. Adult classes, small-faith communities, mid-week Bible studies and neighborhood discussion groups will find these books a helpful resource for in-depth exploration, personal growth and community building. When used in a group, leadership may be designated or shared.

Each of the studies' twelve sections begins with a brief synopsis of the passage and a *Find the Facts* section, which can help you prepare to consider the material. Informative commentary is not intended to provide definitive answers to the meaning of the passage, but to give you background information, clues to the context and suggestions for thought. It can serve as a point of departure for personal reflection or group discussion.

The questions posed in each section are designed to speak to at a variety of levels:

- Some are questions of *interpretation*: What is the author's meaning in this passage?

- Some are questions of *application*: How does the author's message apply to contemporary Christianity?

- Some are questions of *reflection*: How is this God's message to me? to my family? to our community?

Every level contributes to the faith-nurturing impact of the study. The variety of questions are grouped together topically so that you can respond to the level most directly pertaining to your situation. The same goes for group use: participants can respond to those questions most relevant to their current circumstance.

Each section includes suggested *Group Activities*. These activities provide small groups with experiential activities that can help participants to grasp an idea through various methods of learning rather than through intellect alone. These activities involve the whole person—senses, emotions, mind and spirit. If you are using this book in a group setting, we encourage you to incorporate these activities into your group's time together. Many adults may feel awkward when invited to work with clay or pipe cleaners, or to create songs or poetry; they may feel these are childish activities. Such concrete experiences, however, can serve to move group members from learning about an idea toward an understanding of the idea.

Each section closes with a *Journal Meditation* and a *Stepstone to Prayer*. These offer you the opportunity to record or illustrate thoughts and feelings about the passage explored and to express these to God in prayer. The *Journal Meditation* invites you into deep, personal reflection that can produce life-changing understanding. *Stepstone to Prayer* leads you into a time of communion with God.

Individual Use

• Begin each session with prayer—that you will be open to God's message to you, that the Spirit will illuminate God's work, and that you will be empowered to follow God's call.

• Read the passage several times in the scripture translation of your choice. (Note that the New Revised Standard Version Bible has been used in the preparation of these studies.) Try to understand what the author is saying before you begin to interpret, apply or reflect on the message.

• Note key words or phrases that you find especially significant in the scripture. When you have finished a section, go back and review these words or phrases and explore their importance in light of your greater understanding of the passage.

• Spread your exploration of any given section over several days; come back to those question that have provoked considerable thought. You may be surprised at the new insights you find if you spend some time each day on the passage. Give the passage time to sink into your heart and mind.

• Record your thoughts in the space provided. The discipline of journaling can help you synthesize your thoughts and direct your understanding.

Small Group Use

- Prepare for each gathering following the suggestions given above under "Individual Use." Group interaction is impoverished if participants have not immersed themselves in the passage before meeting.

- Begin your time together with prayer. Expect God to increase your faith, expand your understanding of scripture and build your fellowship.

- Accept one another's experiences and interpretations of the passage. Listen carefully to comments; offer your own insights; be willing to look at things in new ways.

Small Group Leadership

- Prepare for each gathering as a participant first. Your role as a leader is not to teach but to facilitate the process of sharing and discovery for everyone.

- Keep in mind the group's time restraints. Begin and end on time. Underline those questions that you think will be most appropriate for your group's discussion time, but be open to those questions that group members wish to pursue.

- Choose one or two group activities that your group will enjoy and learn from. Make sure you have gathered any required materials for your chosen group activities.

- Begin and close each gathering with prayer. Ask a volunteer to read each section of the passage as you come to it in the study.

- Welcome all contributions, but keep the discussion on track. Certain passages may have two or three possible interpretations. Do not be concerned if all participants do not agree in their understanding. Acknowledge the differences of opinion and move on to the next question.

- Allow time at the end of each gathering for those individuals who wish to share their thoughts or drawings from their *Journal Meditations*.

- If your group members are not well-acquainted, it may take some time to build a trust level within the group. Let the dynamics of the group develop as group members gain confidence in themselves and in one another.

Introduction to the Gospel of John

EACH GOSPEL HAS BEEN SYMBOLIZED throughout the centuries by a different animal. John's symbol, the eagle, was given precisely because of the gospel's soaring language as well as keen insights into the meaning of Jesus' words and the spiritual application of Jesus' works. Less of a biographical account of Jesus' life and ministry, the Gospel of John offers an interpretive account by one who had meditated long under the guidance of the Spirit about the significance of Jesus' good news.

The first three gospels, Matthew, Mark and Luke, sometimes referred to as the synoptics, were written from a viewpoint similar to one another and report many of the same incidents from Jesus' life. The Gospel of John, however, is the gospel that is different, and we are all the richer for that difference.

Authorship and Date

We cannot state positively who wrote this gospel, but from very early times, John, the son of Zebedee and one of the twelve apostles, has been accepted as the author. John is presumed to be "the disciple whom Jesus loved" who is first introduced by that title in 13:23, and who also appears at the foot of the cross in 19:26, at the empty tomb in 20:1-8 and by the Sea of Tiberias in 21:7, 20. He is usually thought to be the "other disciple" who helped Peter gain admission to the high priest's courtyard in 18:16. This beloved disciple says he is the one "testifying to these things" (that is, to message and identity of Jesus Christ) in 21:24.

While scholars have raised some questions about the identity of the author, there is no compelling reason to reject the assumption that John the apostle did indeed write—or at least provide the information for—this gospel. We shall, for the purposes of this study, refer to the writer as "John" and accept the theory that he is John the apostle.

It is generally agreed that this gospel was probably composed about A.D. 90–100 and written in Ephesus. This late date makes it the last gospel to be written. John may or may not have had the other gospel accounts before him as he wrote; certainly many of Jesus' teachings and miracles were commonly known by then and, if he was indeed one of the twelve disciples, his writing reflects not just his observations of the events, but his long meditation on their implications.

Purpose

By the end of the first century in the Christian era, there was a need for a fresh statement of the Christian faith. Christianity had been born in the cradle of Judaism, but as that first century drew near its close, Christianity had spread well beyond the Jews and was increasingly a religion of Gentiles. The Gospel of John, written with the Gentile in mind, provided the fresh restatement of the faith built on the words and work of Jesus Christ.

Though the author sought to make his message intelligible to the philosophical Greek, it clearly arises out of a deep understanding of and appreciation for Jewish history and faith. The stated purpose of the work is given in 20:31—"these are written so that you may come to believe that Jesus is the Messiah, the Son of God, and that through believing you may have life in his name." In reading this record of Jesus' words and deeds, both Jew and Gentile alike are called to belief, not only a decision of conversion, but a continual process of believing.

He is true to this stated purpose as he writes. Of all the material on the life and work of Jesus available to him, he selects certain events and words as evidence or "signs" that Jesus is the Messiah promised in the Old Testament and is the Son of God.

John frequently uses courtroom language, and many of those whom Jesus touched give "testimony" in support of John's claim about Jesus. That "Jesus is the Messiah" becomes irrefutably clear throughout the gospel.

John and the Other Gospels

Even a casual reading of John reveals significant differences from the synoptic gospels:

- Jesus speaks very little about "the kingdom of God," preferring instead to teach about the quality of eternal life. He also speaks much more about his own role as an agent of the Father.

- Instead of parables, fairly lengthy speeches of Jesus are recorded.

- John reports seven miracles of Jesus, five of which are found only in John. Also, in John these miracles function as "signs," or divine revelations of Jesus' identity.

• In John a great deal of Jesus' ministry occurs in Judea, primarily in Jerusalem. In the other gospels, Galilee is the normal setting. John begins his gospel by setting Jesus in a theological rather than a historical context (1:1–18). The gospel offers no background to Jesus' human origins or birth and concentrates instead on his spiritual/divine origin.

It is important that John not be viewed as a contradiction of the other three gospels. Rather, we can thank John for providing us with additional information about Jesus and a different point of view from which to see him.

Structure

The following is a simple outline of the gospel:

1:1-18 the prologue, an introduction of the titles and interpretations of Jesus to be used throughout the gospel
1:19–12 Jesus' ministry to the public, displaying his signs to all and teaching about his work
13–17 Jesus' private ministry to the disciples, teaching them the nature of their relationship with him, with the Father and with the Holy Spirit
18–19 the arrest and crucifixion
20 the resurrection
21 an epilogue

Contemporary Relevance

John's gospel continues to be important today because in it we find the clearest statement of who the Church understands Jesus to be. In reading this gospel we also learn a great deal about the work of the Holy Spirit, who can be described as Jesus' "alter ego." Since it is through the Holy Spirit, the presence of the risen Christ within us, that we most frequently meet God today, this gospel serves to help us understand the ways in which the Holy Spirit ministers to us.

Above all, this gospel challenges us, as it challenged the first readers, to believe that Jesus is the Son of God, and that by believing we may inherit eternal life.

John 1–2
Jesus—The Incarnate Word

I**N THESE FIRST TWO CHAPTERS OF THE GOSPEL,** Jesus is first introduced from a spiritual point of view, then as the Christ to whom
John the Baptist points, and finally from the perspective of the
first disciples. John also reports Jesus' first miracle and his clash with the
money-changers and merchants in the temple. Most importantly, John
introduces words that he later develops as primary themes through the
rest of the book. Read through both chapters 1 and 2 at one sitting to
understand the scope of John's introduction.

Find the Facts

Whom does John believe Jesus to be? When did Jesus Christ the Lord
come into being? What is the role of John the Baptist? Who are the first
two disciples identified in this gospel? What need did Jesus meet in his
first miracle? Why was Jesus angry at the merchants in the temple?

1. *Unlike Matthew, Mark and Luke, John begins his account with a beautiful and moving hymn to Jesus' glory. Choose three or four words that John uses in 1:1-18 that describe the essence of Jesus.*

John 1:1-3

Verses 1-18 of chapter 1 are often called John's prologue, for they preface the body of his gospel as a doxology, revealing both Jesus' divine source and his human origin and placing him in a timeless perspective. Rather than starting with Jesus' birth, John returns to Genesis. "In the beginning..." reads GENESIS 1:1, and that is where John places Jesus. This gospel, then, becomes a new creation story, the account of a new beginning in God's relationship with humanity.

John calls Jesus the "Word." The term *word* in Greek thought meant the controlling and organizing force in the world, the higher mind that held everything together. In Jewish thought, *word* represented the creative power of God. In the creation story (GEN. 1), everything came into being through God's word. God speaking is synonymous with God acting creatively. Each of the six creation days begins with the phrase, "and God *said*..."

John's choice of the word *logos* perfectly combines Greek and Hebrew thought and introduces Jesus to both cultures as the fullest expression of the depths of God.

2. *In your own words express what you think is John's main point in 1:1-3.*

3. *What does John's claim about Jesus in 1:1-3 add to your understanding of Jesus? What does it clarify? What questions does it raise?*

John 1:4-5

Light and *life* are key words in John's gospel. He uses them together here in verse 4 and many times more throughout the gospel. This life is different from the period of human existence we call a "life span." Rather, the life in Jesus has about it the essence of "Godness." He does not just *have* life, he *is* life. The eternal life that characterizes God's existence also characterizes the Word.

Jesus is a light to humankind. Powers loose in the world try to hide the life of God in the same way that darkness makes objects difficult to see. Jesus is light because his life and ministry illuminate the life of God so that we may perceive and receive that life.

In speaking of light, John again links Jesus with the creation story. When the earth was "a formless void" (GEN. 1:2), there was only darkness, chaos and disorder. God's first creative act was to bring light.

"Then God said, 'Let there be light'" (Gᴇɴ. 1:3). In the same way, the light of Jesus drives away the chaos of spiritual darkness.

In John's day, light and darkness were not considered simply neutral qualities. Darkness was not just the absence of light; it was a force that was actively hostile to the light of God.

Consider:

4. *What kinds of darkness in the world try to overcome the life of God today? In what circumstances have you observed that darkness is unable to overcome the life of God?*

5. *In what sense do you experience the life of God as light? What kinds of darkness are hostile to the life of God in you?*

John 1:6-8

John the Baptist has a critical role in preparing the people to receive Jesus' message. It is he who serves as the link between the Old Testament prophecies and the new kingdom that dawned with Jesus. John, the writer, takes great pains to put to rest any idea that John the Baptist is himself Christ. Rather, he prepares the way for Jesus.

Besides his role of preparer, John the Baptist serves as a "witness to testify to the light." Throughout the Gospel of John, witnesses come forth to testify concerning Jesus. John the Baptist is called as the first witness and later in this chapter (1:19-28) he is even "interrogated."

As a witness, John the Baptist points to Jesus—to his identity, to his message and to his mission (1:29-37). In the line of the Old Testament prophets before him, John the Baptist calls men and women to repentance, which prepares the way for belief.

Consider:

6. *In what ways is the ministry of John the Baptist a witness and a model for Christians today? How can you help to prepare the way for Jesus in someone else's life? Who would you call the preparer in your life?*

John 1:9-18

When John says of Jesus that "the world did not know him," he explains a purpose for writing. Though the creating force of the universe resides in Jesus, people fail to recognize him. To miss meeting Jesus is tragic, so John writes to give people the evidence they need to see Jesus. Though Jesus' exhortation to be "born from above" comes later (3:3), John introduces this thought here. By receiving Jesus, we experience God's power (1:12), enabling us to inherit a position of privilege as God's children.

"And the Word became flesh and lived among us, full of grace and truth." John summarizes the Christmas story in this one sentence. The birth narratives from Matthew and Luke are useful in telling us what *happened* on the first Christmas, but John tells us what that day *means*. Like Matthew, John understands the incarnation as the presence of God among humanity (Mt. 1:23), surpassing every other experience in the history of God's chosen people. In Jesus, God is with us more fully than ever before (Ex. 40:34-38). The glory of the Lord manifests itself clearly in Jesus, explicitly in the transfiguration (which John possibly alludes to in 1:14) and implicitly in his ministry (2:11).

Grace and *truth*, two weighty words in John's gospel, perfectly describe this incarnate Word. Grace describes that unmerited favor of God, which Jesus embodies and communicates to us. Though the word *grace* never appears again in John's gospel, its presence here alerts us to watch for God's favor in all that Jesus says and does.

Truth becomes a refrain throughout the gospel. It describes the reality that lies behind all the confusion, misbelief and ignorance of our lives. In Hebrew thought, truth only had meaning in relation to God's character; the reality of God provided the basis for truth, and God's name represented the integrity of truth (Is. 45:19, 65:16; Ps. 43:3, 51:6). For John, Jesus does more than simply tell us the truth; Jesus the Word *is* truth (14:6; Eph. 4:21).

Here John honors Moses' role as the giver of the law, but elevates Jesus in comparison. Moses told us how to conform our lives to God's truth; Jesus came to impart God's truth.

Consider:

7. John says of Jesus, "we have seen his glory" (1:14). Do you think the "we" he was speaking of refers only to those who were eye-witnesses of Jesus in the flesh? Why or why not? How is Jesus' glory eternally present in our world today?

John 1:19-3

Many Jews of Jesus' day anxiously awaited their deliverer, their Messiah ("the Anointed One of God," Gk., *Christ*). A fiery leader like John the Baptist, who apparently rallied the people, might well have become such a deliverer.

Refusing any misdirected devotion, John the Baptist claims that he is neither the Messiah, Elijah nor the prophet. Through Malachi, God had promised to send the great Jewish hero, Elijah, who had not died (2 KG. 2:11), to prepare the people for the day of the Lord, the day of final judgment and the fulfillment of God's promised salvation (MAL. 4:5-6).

Though John the Baptist ministered "with the spirit and power of Elijah" (LK. 1:17) and thereby acted in a fulfillment of this prophecy (MT. 11:14, 17:10-13), he was not Elijah. Neither was he the promised prophet-like-Moses (DT. 18:17-18). Quoting from another great prophet, Isaiah, John the Baptist calls himself the preparer (Is. 40:3); the one who makes all things ready for a greater one.

John the Baptist then identifies Jesus as that One, the Lamb of God. Such a title recalls the sacrificial lamb slaughtered at Passover. Passover is the feast that celebrates the Israelites' deliverance from Egypt when the blood of lambs caused the angel of death to pass over God's people (Ex. 12:1-14).

Consider:

8. *If you had been standing next to John the Baptist (1:29), what would you have felt and understood by "Here is the Lamb of God who takes away the sin of the world"? In what way does Jesus take away sin in the world today?*

John 1:35-51

One of the most obvious facts about the response of these first followers of Jesus is that meeting him inspired them to tell somebody else. Andrew told Simon; Philip told Nathanael. Presumably each of these four then told others. The coming of Jesus was good news, and the natural response to good news is to tell someone else.

Consider the obstacles these men had to overcome to believe that Jesus was the Son of God. Certainly skepticism and doubt were present. Nathanael also had to overcome his prejudice about Nazareth, an obscure town in northern Palestine. But when Simon and Nathanael came to see Jesus for themselves, they were convinced and followed Jesus. Simon received a new name (Peter, "rock"), the promise of rebirth. Nathanael received a commendation from one who had looked into his soul. (A fig tree was a favorite shady place for personal prayer.)

Consider:

9. *In what ways is the presence of Jesus in your life good news? Does this news inspire you to share it? What things make the good news difficult to share? How can we overcome these difficulties?*

10. *What obstacles hinder you in your Christian faith journey? Is there a way in which you can "come and see" for yourself?*

John 2:1-12

John's account of Jesus' first miracle serves as another witness to support his claim that Jesus is the Son of God. Mary, too, "gives testimony"; in bringing her concern to Jesus, she discloses her confidence in Jesus' unique abilities.

In the Jewish culture of Jesus' day, a wedding was the occasion for a grand celebration, often lasting up to a week. Hospitality played a major role in eastern societies, and a wedding was often a critical measure of a family's hospitality. The lack of a sufficient supply of wine for the guests caused more than chagrin; it was a social disgrace. Jesus' gracious gesture demonstrates "his glory" and is the first of the seven "signs" John records. Each miracle in the gospel becomes a window through which the seeker can see the truth of Jesus. This sign in particular reveals Jesus' supremacy over the law, represented by the stone jars used in the Jewish purification rites. The law prescribed cleansing from every variety of defilement (Mk. 7:3-4), but was powerless to provide new life, as symbolized by the wine (Gen. 27:28; Num. 18:12; Dt. 7:13, 33:28; Jer. 31:12).

Not only did Jesus' action demonstrate the failure of the old covenant of the law, it proclaimed the unsurpassable abundance of the new covenant of Jesus (10:10). That much superior wine (120-180 gallons) would provide for weeks and weeks of celebration. Jesus' message was one of lavish grace (Eph. 1:7-8).

Consider:

11. *Of what is this first miracle a sign for you? Explain your answer. To what event in your life would you like to invite Jesus and his disciples? What miracle do you need Jesus to perform?*

12. What is the significance in this story of the role of Mary? of the servants? of the steward? What part have you played in someone else's miracles? How has it revealed Jesus' glory and increased someone's faith?

John 2:13-25

The incident of the clash with the money-changers in the temple is also reported by the other three gospel writers, but each of them place the incident during the final week of Jesus' earthly life. John, on the other hand, puts it early in Jesus' ministry. Instead of writing a chronologically arranged biography of Jesus, John reported selected incidents that supported the claim that Jesus was the Son of God.

The practice of selling animals for sacrifice probably arose innocently enough. The temple in Jerusalem was the only acceptable place for sacrifice, and pious Jews from all parts of the ancient world would travel to Jerusalem to fulfill their religious duties.

An animal chosen for sacrifice must be unblemished (Lev. 1:10, 3:6, 4:3). Spotless at the start of a long journey, an animal would rarely be found without defect by the time the traveler reached Jerusalem. Appointed temple officials inspected each animal at a cost to the worshiper; if it were rejected, another would have to be purchased.

By the time of Jesus, these officials had probably become corrupt, rejecting most animals and charging exorbitant prices for acceptable ones. The abuse was compounded by the monetary exchange system of the temple. Only temple currency was accepted in the purchase and inspection of the animals, and the money-changers made a great profit by offering a poor exchange rate.

All of this business was being conducted in the outer courts of the temple, which was the only place Gentile "God-fearers" could worship. Instead of being "a light to the nations" (Is. 42:6, 49:6), Israel's religious center had become a marketplace.

Jesus passionately opposes this abuse. His violent demonstration of outrage calls forth the first signs of hostility from the Jewish leaders. They demand a sign of his credentials. Again and again they ask for proof (4:48, 6:30, 10:24), but reject the signs he provides (2:23). Here Jesus alludes to the ultimate sign of his authority—his death and resurrection. The temple, representative of the old covenant of the law, will indeed be destroyed and a new one raised (Rev. 21:22).

Consider:

13. What does the incident in the temple reveal to you about Jesus? How do you feel about the power and emotion expressed? In what sense might Jesus operate in a similar fashion today? in the world? in the Church? in your life?

14. What habits in your spiritual life might be keeping you from pure worship and from being a light to others?

Group Activities

1. Distribute drawing paper and crayons and invite group members to express JOHN 1:1-5 as a drawing. When these are completed, invite volunteers to show their drawings.

   Allow group members to discuss the feelings that each of the drawings raises.

   What reassuring feelings are expressed? what empowering feelings? what feelings of worship?

2. List on a chalkboard or newsprint the various pieces of evidence that Jesus is God's Son and each of the "witnesses" that John offers.

   Ask group members to imagine that they are on trial for claiming that Jesus is the Son of God. What personal witness could they offer to support their claim?

   Have group members imagine that they are attorneys and decide how they would arrange the evidence that John provides for a presentation in Jesus' defense.

3. Ask the group to identify the various words and titles used for Jesus in the first two chapters of John. List these on chalkboard or newsprint.

   Discuss the different aspects of Jesus that each title suggests:
   • In what ways do these words and titles reveal Jesus' divinity?
   • How do they define his mission?

4. Provide for group members a variety of the following materials: clay, aluminum foil, pipe cleaners, watercolors (and brushes), drawing paper, charcoal pencils, etc. Ask each group member to select one of the words or titles for Jesus that they listed above (or take time to list them now) and to illustrate it using one or more of the materials listed. Invite volunteers to explain their work.

Journal Meditation

John says of Jesus that "we have seen his glory, the glory as of a father's only Son" (1:14). Take a few moments to think about the ways in which you have "seen the glory" of Jesus. Try to remember how such beholding made you feel. Then record here any insight that this remembering brings, whether about Jesus, about yourself or about your relationship with others.

Stepstone to Prayer

"We have found the Messiah." And Jesus said, "Follow me."

John 3–5
The Beginning of Jesus' Ministry

3/2/08

THIS PORTION OF THE GOSPEL REPORTS JESUS' encounters with four people. Jesus' ministry to individuals not only demonstrated his power, but offered evidence of his intensely personal care for each person. Perhaps more than any other gospel writer, John invites his readers into a close relationship with Jesus like those so tenderly portrayed in his conversations with people in need.

The four individuals were a varied group. One was a high-ranking Jew, a Pharisee. Another was from the dregs of Jewish society. A third was a woman of loose morals who belonged to a race hated by the Jews. The fourth was possibly a Roman who held an important government position. John shows that Jesus bridges the barriers that often separate people.

Jesus follows these events with a discourse on the relationship between the Father and the Son. Read JOHN 3–5.

Find the Facts

Which two encounters does Jesus initiate? Which events in these chapters take place in Judea? which in Samaria? which in Galilee? What new testimony about Jesus does John the Baptist offer? What metaphor does the Baptist use to describe his relationship to Jesus?

1. *No doubt Jesus spoke one-on-one with many more individuals than those mentioned by the four gospel writers. Why do you think John selected these four encounters to include in his gospel?*

2. *Jesus frequently refers to God as "the Father," yet Jesus tells the Samaritan woman that "God is spirit" (4:24). In what ways does this latter description suggest an image of God that is more universal than the term "Father" conveys? How might the "God is spirit" image be a useful one for our day?*

John 3:1-21

The Pharisees, a religious sect, devoted themselves to a strict adherence to the Old Testament laws, including the several hundred rabbinical interpretations of those laws. This legalistic approach to life set the Pharisees as a whole in conflict with Jesus, who taught that the law was best fulfilled by loving God and one's neighbor (MT. 22:34-40; MK. 12:28-34; ROM. 13:8).

Thus for Nicodemus to come to Jesus at all is remarkable. His visit reveals that the legalistic approach to life is less than satisfying for him; he wants something more. He comes with sincere questions and seems willing to consider a fresh understanding of life. Given his Pharisaical training, he no doubt found Jesus' words mind-boggling.

Nicodemus recognizes the purpose of the signs—to point us to God in Jesus. His questioning takes the form of a statement, but Jesus responds on an entirely different level. He confronts Nicodemus at his point of greatest strength. As a Jew, Nicodemus' security lay in his relationship with God as defined by the covenant, the law, and the prophets. The truth of God had only been revealed to the Jews, for they were God's chosen people. The Gentiles were the ones who had to worry about getting into God's kingdom.

Yet Jesus' words challenge Nicodemus, forcing him to reconsider his position before God. On what was his righteousness based? on his genetic make-up? on his careful observance of the law? Everyone must begin again, Jesus says. One way to understand the kingdom of God is to view it as a spiritual reality present to all persons. However, only those who diligently look for God's plan for life can recognize the kingdom. Kingdom values so differ from the values of the world that to enter this kingdom of God is like being born all over again.

Many old values die as the new values of God's kingdom emerge. When a person is born anew in this way, that person can then see the kingdom of God. Jesus also introduces the sovereign work of the Spirit, who renews each person as dramatically as a tempest, or as indiscernibly as a gentle breeze.

Jesus' reference to the serpent in the wilderness recalls the Israelites' homelessness before they entered God's promised land. Often they forgot their total dependence on God's goodness. At one point they were punished by poisonous snakes. At God's direction, Moses posted a bronze image of a snake on a pole. By looking at the snake, the poisoned people lived (NUM. 21:4-9). This unusual story illustrates Jesus' work in being lifted up on a cross.

Verse 16 is, perhaps, one of the most-memorized and best-loved verses of scripture, for it contains the essence of the Christian faith that affirms the existence of a personal God whose attitude toward creation is one of love. The Son is now the pivotal point of all existence, and our relationship with the Son saves or condemns us. The Son brings light into a darkened world, but some prefer the obscurity of evil.

3. Nicodemus' Pharisaic legalism kept him from coming to Jesus openly. What kinds of legalism inhibit people from coming openly to Jesus today? What examples of legalism do you see at work in your dealings with others? with yourself?

4. In what sense do you feel wind aptly describes being born of the Spirit? What is your experience with such a wind?

5. Read Luke 17:21, Matthew 4:17 and Matthew 13:44. What do each of these say about the kingdom of God? How do they contribute to an understanding of Jesus' words in 3:3?

John 3:22-36

As in 1:19-28, John the Baptist again emphasizes that he is not the main event but plays a supporting role. Jesus is the bridegroom; John the Baptist is the bridegroom's friend, the best man. Though the best man may serve a significant role, this role diminishes when the bride and groom wed. Verses 31-36 continue the gospel writer's reflections on the identify of Jesus and the relevance of his message to our world. The one who rejects the Son does not escape God's wrath.

Consider:

6. *If Jesus is the groom, and John the best man, who is the bride? Reflect on the feelings of John the Baptist and his disciples. How would you feel if such popularity and reputation were slipping from you? Why was John calm and self-effacing in this situation?*

7. *In what ways must we decrease while Jesus increases? How does this decrease relate to the contemporary call to self-affirmation? Does this decrease support the concept of self-denial? Why or why not?*

John 4:1-15

There had been bad blood between the Jews and the Samaritans for several centuries. The Samaritans were descendants of those Jews who had remained in Palestine when the Assyrians marched most of the people of the northern kingdom of Israel away into captivity. These Jews who remained behind eventually intermarried with people of other nations whom the Assyrians forcibly resettled in Palestine. To the pure Jews of Judah, intermarriage with non-Jews was unforgivable. The Samaritans were also despised because their worship was viewed by Jews as a corrupted form of Jewish rituals.

Though Jesus wished to return to Galilee, he did not have to go through Samaria. Though Samaria lay between Judea and Galilee, most Jews traveled the longer route around Samaria, thereby avoiding contact; Jesus purposely traveled through Samaria. In speaking to the woman at the well, Jesus defied convention and invited ostracism. In that male-dominated society, the disciples "were astonished" that Jesus would speak publicly with a woman at all (4:27).

In the discussion about water, Jesus offers *living* water. The woman assumes he means *running* water, as from a stream, and wonders about its source. Gradually this woman begins to understand that what Jesus offers is not something to assuage physical thirst, but the grace of God that satisfies the thirst to be made whole.

8. *What words would you use to describe the tone of Jesus' encounter with the woman at the well? The woman was bound by what she understood of her spiritual tradition (4:12). In what ways does Jesus challenge us to break out of comfortable traditions and into the living waters of his life? (See Lk. 5:36-39).*

9. *The Jews despised the Samaritans as an inferior race. The woman received even more scorn because of her immoral past. What forces encourage this kind of bias today? What helps combat this kind of attitude? In what ways does Jesus' message transcend physical, moral and spiritual prejudices?*

John 4:16-26

This conversation between Jesus and the woman now turns to the nature of true worship. The woman raises the issue regarding the proper location for worship, a subject of much debate between the Jews and the Samaritans. The Jews considered Jerusalem and the temple there as the focal point for the worship of God; the Samaritans revered Mt. Gerizim, near where she and Jesus stand, as the sacred spot.

Jesus answers the woman by moving the whole matter of worship into a larger arena. True worship is not a matter of location or authorized ritual; it is an attitude of the heart and a humble willingness to follow the truth. Throughout the gospel, truth resides in Jesus (14:6) and he freely states that he is the Messiah, the bearer of the truth.

Consider:

10. *Jesus reproved the woman for worshiping in ignorance. In what ways has your worship been uninformed? lifeless? To what can you attribute this?*

11. *How does the place where you worship affect the quality of your worship? In what ways are you influenced by ritual, music, the personality of the worship leader and other external components of public worship? In what ways do you worship in spirit and in truth?*

John 4:27-42

In this passage, John describes an interesting progression leading to belief. Overwhelmed by her meeting with Jesus, the woman still has doubts about his identity as the Messiah. In the village, she spreads the word about this remarkable man that she has met, but does so with a question: "Can this be the Christ?"

Her report is enough to bring other Samaritans out to the well, and some of them believe because of the woman's testimony regarding Jesus' knowledge of her life. But in the end, they believe because of meeting Jesus himself (4:42). These Samaritans also become witnesses to Jesus' identity: "...this is indeed the Savior of the world."

Consider:

12. *What impact did Jesus have on the woman? on her city? Why? Whose testimony about an encounter with Jesus helped to bring you to faith in Jesus? What does your testimony about Jesus consist of?*

John 4:43-54

We come now to the third significant encounter contained in today's scripture. John uses this story to demonstrate Jesus' power over illness and to highlight the superiority of faith that is not the result of mind-dazzling wonders. Jesus challenges the official's faith, but the man persists, thereby demonstrating that his faith is not easily shaken and will not be turned away. John calls this healing the second of Jesus' signs (2:11), but the official believed in Jesus before he saw the sign. John wants his readers to do the same.

13. *What is the significance of the man's learning the hour of his son's healing? If he had not received this information, what difference might it have made to him? to you? React to this statement in light of this passage: "Faith is not being sure where you're going but going anyway" (Frederick Buechner).*

John 5:1-18

Before healing the man, Jesus asks him about his desire for healing. It is an important question, for not everyone wants to hear the good news Jesus brings. John makes it clear that, though Jesus comes as a light in the darkness of this world (1:5), some people prefer darkness because of the evil of their lives (3:19-20). The question echoes John's assertion that those who choose to receive Jesus are empowered to become God's children.

John points out that this healing took place on the sabbath and that both the work of healing performed by Jesus and the work of carrying the pallet done by the healed man were violations of the Pharisaical interpretations of the law. Though Jesus was not a law-breaker, some perceived him as such. The compassion of God, flowing through Jesus' actions, could not be contained in the narrow confines of a religious system that had missed the main point.

Verse 4 is omitted from more ancient manuscripts. It explains why the sick would lay beside the pool: "For an angel of the Lord went down at certain seasons into the pool, and stirred up the water; whoever stepped in first after the stirring of the water was made well from whatever disease that person had."

14. *Imagine the despairing scene that surrounded the man by the pool and the hopelessness that must have filled him. How would you have responded to Jesus' question in verse 6? Do you ever not want to be "made well"? In what ways do we sometimes resist obvious solutions to our difficulties? Why?*

15. *What do you think Jesus' warning in verse 14 referred to? Why?*

John 5:19-47

In this discourse, Jesus plainly defines the relationship between the Father and himself, indicating that his authority comes from God who sent him. In addition to identifying himself as the Son of God, Jesus also appropriates the title "Son of Man" (5:27), an Old Testament term (DAN. 7:13) for one who would come as a Messiah.

Earlier Jesus praised the faith of the non-Jewish Capernaum official. Here in verses 45-47 he expresses concern that the Jews, who have the advantage of knowing the scriptures, will have far less faith, believing neither the scriptures nor him. Moses, their spiritual hero, would in the end accuse them of unbelief, for in Moses' writings, the Pentateuch (Genesis, Exodus, Leviticus, Numbers and Deuteronomy) the Messiah was promised. (See GEN. 3:15; NUM. 24:17; DT. 18:17-19.)

16. *On what grounds can we expect to gain eternal life? Why? How do you think the refusal to come to Jesus is linked with the absence of the love of God (5:40, 42)?*

17. *John shows that both the Father, Moses and scripture witness to Jesus' identity. We too have the scriptures. How do we know they are a reliable witness to Jesus as the Son of God?*

Group Activities

1. Post a large map of Palestine in Jesus' time. Identify the three major regional divisions of that day: Galilee, Samaria and Judea. Using your Bibles, and beginning at JOHN 1:28, trace Jesus' movements up through the end of today's reading. When cities or other specific locations are named in John, locate these on the map. Try to discover, using the evidence in the scripture, what things prompted Jesus' movements.

2. Ask one member of the group to roleplay the invalid man by the pool of Bethzatha. After rereading JOHN 5:2-9, ask the person doing the roleplay to tell his or her "history" as an invalid, to enumerate the problems caused and the sympathy received because of the handicap, and then deal with the question "Do you want to be healed?" At the end of the roleplay, invite the

other members of the group to comment on anything they saw in the portrayal with which they can identify.

3. Review the four people we met in this study:
   - Nicodemus—an upper-class Jew
   - the man at the pool—a lower-class Jew
   - the woman at the well—a Samaritan with a bad reputation
   - the Capernaum official—an important Roman

   Using evidence from the gospel, ask the group to name the most striking personality characteristic of each of these. Finally, ask four group members to volunteer to "adopt" the four people from today's scripture and then "introduce" their adoptees to the rest of the group. Tell whatever history is needed (this can be made up) to enable the group to understand what made these persons ready to hear Jesus' good news.

4. Distribute colored chalk and drawing paper. Invite group members to reflect on the following: "Faith is having all your windows open to God's wind" (George MacDonald). Invite group members to illustrate the ways they have experienced the wind of the Spirit in their lives.

Journal Meditation

Recall a time when events in your life made you ready to hear the good news. Think about how troubles sometimes make you more open to God. Recalling these important times may open you to God afresh. Listen for what God says to you now and record your thoughts and feelings in the space below.

Stepstone to Prayer

Jesus, I am standing beside the well of Samaria. I see you approaching. I feel...

John 6
Believing Is Seeing

IN THIS CHAPTER, JESUS RAISES THE ISSUE OF BELIEF, which he identifies as the key to eternal life. What we believe about Jesus determines our relationship with God, as John summarizes in 20:31.

John has already indicated the importance of belief in 3:16-18, but in chapter 6 he clarifies this theme: to see Jesus for who he is, we must believe, and the fruit of believing is eternal life.

Jesus' feeding of the five thousand provides an opportunity for Jesus to explain his role as the bread of life, heavenly nourishment from God for all who hunger. Read JOHN 6.

Find the Facts

Which disciple was "tested" by Jesus during the feeding of the five thousand? What are the two names of the body of water upon which Jesus walked? Why did the people follow Jesus to the other shore? What hunger does the bread of God satisfy? What caused many of the disciples to draw back and follow Jesus no more?

[Handwritten margin notes:]

VS. 4 Feast of Passover was near.

9 - five barley loaves and two fishes but what good are these for so many?

19 - Jesus walking on water

29 - This is the work of God, that you believe in the One he sent.

35 - I am the Bread of Life

48 - I am the Bread of Life

Jesus takes initiative in synoptics disciples do

eating his flesh & blood

Ex. 16:2 7-8 "people murmuring"

Andrew

Sea of Galilee

Job 9:8 God "treads upon the crests of the sea."

"walking on the sea" or "by the sea"

Greek could mean "on the seashore" or "by the water"

parallels - esp. Mt. 14:25 walked upon the water make clear Jesus walked upon the water

1. *Sometimes we can tell which issues a gospel writer considers most important by the repetition of certain words. What four or five words or phrases are used frequently in this chapter? Which ones seem especially important to a proper understanding of Jesus? Why?*

2. *John reports several incidents in this chapter. Write one sentence that you think synthesizes the events and summarizes John's purpose in recording them.*

John 6:1-13

Since it was near the Jewish festival of Passover, the crowds around Jesus were probably bigger than ever; pilgrims en route to Jerusalem for the Passover no doubt joined the local people who pressed near Jesus.

Though it is likely that Jesus' had retreated to be alone with the disciples, he expresses no resentment when the crowds appeared. His first concern is to feed them, much like the concern of a householder who has just had guests drop in unexpectedly.

John interprets the question posed to Philip as a test, to prove the extent of his faith. Philip's response shows that he is concentrating not on the potential, but on the problem. His remark that two hundred denarii would not buy enough is the equivalent of saying that eight months' wages would be insufficient.

Andrew, who never seems to be a leader among the disciples but who always appears bringing someone to Jesus (1:41, 12:22), tells Jesus of the boy with a small amount of food. This is the only miracle, besides Jesus' resurrection, that all four gospel writers include (MT. 14:13-21; MK. 6:32-44; LK. 9:10-17).

The account perfectly introduces Jesus' discourse on the bread of life in the latter part of the chapter. It also implicitly compares Jesus to Moses, who was much acclaimed in Jewish history as the giver of manna, the miraculous food from heaven. (See Ex. 16:1-5, 11-18, 31-32.) Much like his work of changing the water into wine (2:1-11), Jesus' provision for the needs of the people is a provision of abundance, of overwhelming plenty.

Consider:

3. How do you think that this miracle, the fourth sign, compares with the first sign (2:1-11)? What are the similarities and differences? What does this sign add to your understanding of Jesus?

4. Why do you think all four gospel writers included this miracle?

John 6:14-21

The feeding of the five thousand was considered by the crowds to be a "sign" (6:14) of Jesus' identity. Many people misunderstood the signs, however, and interpreted them in light of their own expectations. Others rejected the signs, even wanting more proof (6:30).

Jesus was never willing to dazzle people into following him by performing miracles to convince them that he was the Son of God. He knew that people who followed him for that reason really would not possess the faith necessary to perceive the kingdom of God. Whenever Jesus did something that could be considered a sign, he did it because some human need or some particular circumstance required it. *N evangelist 7*

When John now points out these signs, it is as if he were saying "Jesus refused to provide signs just to convince you, but for those who were paying attention, plenty of signs were present."

We should not be fooled into thinking that John expects to be convincing simply because he identifies signs. He knows that, in the final analysis, the signs will only be convincing to those who look at them through the lens of faith. No doubt this is why John quotes Jesus' words in verse 36: "But I said to you that you have seen me and yet do not believe." John is fully convinced that belief is not a product of sight. Sight is a product of belief. Believing is seeing. *Not seeing is believing*

John's recounting of the fifth sign is surprisingly short, especially compared with its parallel versions in Matthew 14:22-33 and Mark 6:47-51, and without any accompanying remarks by either John or Jesus. This was a sign reserved exclusively for the disciples, who, after receiving a tremendous shock, also received Jesus' words of intimate comfort, "It is I; do not be afraid."

Many scholars feel that this brief story perfectly prepares Jesus' disciples for the difficult discourse that would follow. In demonstrating his authority over nature (including his own body's density), Jesus may have been effectively revealing his ability to turn up in the most unexpected places.

5. *What signs have been helpful to you in your own search for faith? In what ways has faith diminished the need for signs? In what sense is the statement "believing is seeing" true for you?*

6. *What turbulent times have you experienced in which Jesus approached with words of peace?*

John 6:22-40

The people ate a dinner that Jesus miraculously provided; perhaps now they hope for breakfast. Jesus redirects their focus from their physical needs to their spiritual hunger. He urges them to work for the heavenly food, spiritual nourishment that could sustain their life with God.

The people latch on to his reference to work, for the Jewish leaders had interpreted the law as a system of works that enabled them to achieve righteousness in God's eyes. Perhaps they hope that Jesus would simply give them a list of rules and regulations by which they could earn eternal life.

Unlike any other Jewish rabbi, Jesus provides no such list. There is only one work that God requires: belief in Jesus. In John's gospel, the word believe, however, (Gk., *pisteusate*) means much more than mere acceptance of certain facts about Jesus. It implies an absolute reliance upon him, an acceptance of his message and a participation in his mission.

The other gospel writers emphasize Jesus' teaching on the values prescribed by the kingdom and the kind of lifestyle that should result from those values. (See MT. 5:48; LK. 6:46-49.) John's emphasis on belief does not contradict the message of the other gospels, for John's belief involves a change of direction. "Believe in" may be translated, "believe into"; it is a belief that transforms the believer.

The people compare Jesus to Moses, the lawgiver, who authenticated his authority by bringing bread from heaven (Ex. 16:4). Jesus' claim far surpasses that of Moses, for he does not come simply to bring bread—he is the bread.

Verse 35 records the first of Jesus' seven "I am" statements (8:12, 10:7, 11, 11:25, 14:6, 15:1). Jesus defines himself in each of these statements using a formula ("I am") that is strictly forbidden by the Jews. God had revealed the divine name as I AM (Ex. 3:14) and Jesus' appropriation of those words is no coincidental reference to his divine origin. Each "I am" statement reveals more fully Jesus' identity and mission.

Here Jesus promises that those who come to him will find full spiritual nourishment. They also receive cause for future hope. Though John, perhaps more than the other gospel writers, is more concerned with the present realization of the kingdom within the life of the individual, he does not avoid Jesus' promises about the ultimate fulfillment of that which is now inner and spiritual. The follower of Jesus is promised acceptance, security and finally victory over death.

7. In what ways do you think the Father gives individuals to Jesus? In what sense have you experienced the Father giving you to Jesus?

8. What are the similarities between the bread of God that Jesus offered the crowd and the living water that he offered the woman at the well (4:13-15)?

9. Jesus uses the word will four times in verses 38-40 to express the deepest desire of the Father as reflected in Jesus. In your own words, express what you think the will of the Father is according to this passage. Is this will a comfort to you or a constraint? Why?

10. Eternal life has both a present and a future reality. In what ways do we experience eternal life now? What aspects of eternal life are yet to be experienced?

John 6:41-59

Anyone who seeks to convince others of some matter does well to anticipate the objections the others may raise. In this passage, John records two objections of Jesus' opponents, expecting that his readers may also have the same questions.

Both objections reveal the level at which Jesus' opponents deal with him. They can not, or will not, open themselves to the spiritual realities of which Jesus speaks, preferring to take refuge in the apparent physical obstacles.

Matthew and Luke inform us of Jesus' divine parentage (Mt. 1:18-25; Lk. 1:26-38), but Jesus refuses to divert his teaching by defending his miraculous birth. He explains that those who are drawn to believe in him do so because God opens their spiritual eyes. Such questions would only be answered by faith.

The second obstacle is their physical interpretation of his invitation to eat his flesh and drink his blood. Nothing could be more offensive to a pious Jew to whom human flesh was prohibited, and all blood—human or animal—was holy (Lev. 17:10-12).

Many scholars feel that, since John does not include an account of the Last Supper, this passage contains the essence of that institution. Indeed, no other passage so clearly explains the meaning of the Eu-charist—that by partaking of Jesus' life and death, by fully taking his life into ours, we find life..

It is easy to see the spiritual application in the Eucharist and turn it into yet another sort of literal interpretation. Some may want verse 53 to teach that the sacrament alone can earn eternal life. They may want the Christian life to consist solely in the religious ritual (6:36), thereby continuing in the regulation-minded spirit of Jesus' listeners. Yet it is the spiritual truth behind the physical symbol of the Eucharist that Jesus brings—he is the heavenly nourishment that sustains our relationship with God.

11. *The modern equivalent of the objection raised in verse 42 may be, "Wasn't Jesus really only a human being, a charismatic figure perhaps, but still only a human being?" What kinds of responses might you give to that objection today?*

12. *How would you respond to the question "What does the Eucharist do for you?"*

John 6:60-71

John now tells us that many of the disciples cease following Jesus, finding his sayings too hard. The word *disciple* here refers not solely to the twelve, but to the larger circle of people who follow Jesus. *Disciple* means a learner, or pupil. Many see Jesus as a rabbi, a teacher. The twelve are sometimes called *apostles*, and this term means "one who is commissioned and sent forth." The apostles were also disciples, but not all disciples were apostles. ✳

Some of this larger group of disciples find Jesus' teaching "difficult." This did not just mean that they find what he says difficult to *understand*; it means that they find what he says *hard to accept*. Jesus' words clearly set forth his call to devotion to God through him.

As a result, many desert Jesus. Jesus' words even shake the loyalty of his most intimate companions, the twelve specially called. His claims to a unique relationship with the Father (6:44-46) and an offer of eternal life based on devotion to him (6:29, 35, 51, 53-58) were *skandalon*, offensive. The fact that such teaching is couched in cannibalistic terms makes it even repulsive, a scandal to the Jews, probably an embarrassment to the twelve.

Yet Jesus pushes his disciples, urging them to perceive and to penetrate the spiritual truths behind the literal words. In this difficult discourse, Jesus uses his own flesh and blood, his body, as a living parable to reveal his identity as the source of life and sustenance.

Peter's conclusion echoes throughout the centuries, voicing the thoughts of all seekers of God—where else can we turn? Who else could we follow? only Jesus comes as the Holy One of God.

13. In your own words, what is the meaning of discipleship? What was the cost of discipleship in Jesus' day? What were its demands? What were its rewards? What are the costs, demands and rewards of discipleship today? In what ways are you a disciple? What is Jesus teaching you?

14. What do you do personally find hard about Jesus' sayings? Is there a part of you that wants to draw back from following Jesus? Is there a part that wants to follow him more closely? How do you reconcile these two?

15. How do you think Jesus' comments about flesh and spirit (6:63) might relate to the Eucharist? In what ways is the Eucharist an active parable? How are Jesus' words spirit and life to you?

Group Activities

1. Distribute paper and pens or pencils to the group members. Ask them to rewrite JOHN 6:47-51 in their own words. Then invite group members to read their completed paraphrases to the group.

   Discuss these paraphrases, centering your discussion around the various words that people substitute for "bread of life," "eternal life," "believe," "bread" and "flesh." List these various substituted words on a chalkboard or on newsprint.

   Discuss how these words aid in grasping the intent of Jesus' words in these verses.

2. Instruct group members to close their eyes and imagine that they are part of the crowd that Jesus fed. Then ask the group to identify the sights, sounds and smells that were a part of that imagining. Next ask what they heard Jesus saying as the bread was shared. Point out that imagining ourselves part of any scene where Jesus is present is a valid way of meditating for spiritual growth.

3. Distribute 3" x 5" cards and pens or pencils. Copy the sentences below on chalkboard or newsprint and invite group members to complete each of them:
   - Jesus is a teacher, so I have learned...
   - Jesus is the bread of life, so I have experienced...
   - Jesus has seen God (6:46), so I believe...
   - Jesus said to eat of his flesh and drink of his blood, so I...
   - Jesus is the Son of God, so I...

4. Divide into two groups, assigning one group JOHN 6:1-14 and the other group JOHN 6:15-20. Give each group a sheet of newsprint and a marker. Ask group members to read their respective passages, putting themselves into the scene as eyewitness reporters. Have group members work together to write a headline and brief news report of their story in the style of a local newspaper, a parish newsletter or a newsstand tabloid.

   When finished, have the groups post and read their headlines and stories.

Journal Meditation

Consider some particularly troublesome problem in your life, perhaps one that defies solution. Draw a picture or diagram in the space below to symbolize that problem.

Remember that Jesus came to the 12 at a moment when they were in difficulty and said, "It is I; do not be afraid" (6:20). Take a few moments to close your eyes and imagine how your drawing might change if Jesus spoke those same words to you regarding the problem you have pictured. Now change the drawing as seems appropriate.

Stepstone to Prayer

"Lord, to whom can we go? You have the words of eternal life."

John 7—8
The Growing Opposition

WHAT FORCES LED TO JESUS' DEATH ON THE CROSS? Theologically, we may view Jesus' death as sacrificial. But John also wants his readers to understand that some very human forces engineered Jesus' death. Many people stumbled over Jesus' words, for those words, like light, exposed the evil hiding in the darkness of self-deception.

This study's scripture reports some of the objections people raised against Jesus, as well as his response to those objections. The chapters also report several attempts to arrest and kill Jesus. Read JOHN 7– 8.

Find the Facts

Was Jesus aware of the growing strength of the forces against him? What actions on Jesus' part showed this awareness? Who encouraged Jesus to "go public" at the feast? What feast was being held in Jerusalem at this time? Why didn't Jesus condemn the woman caught in adultery? Who, according to Jesus, are the true children of Abraham? Who accused Jesus of being a Samaritan and of being possessed by a demon?

1. *What three or four words highlight the themes in chapters 7 and 8? Explain your choice of words.*

2. *Which of the words you chose in response to question 1 have been reoccurring themes in John's gospel? Which of these words, do you think, are reoccurring themes in the New Testament as a whole?*

3/16/08

John 7:1-13

The feast of Tabernacles was also known as Sukkot or the feast of Booths. An important annual Jewish festival of the fall season, it originally celebrated God's goodness in the harvest. It also commemorated the time when the people of Israel lived in temporary shelters during their journey in the wilderness after the exodus from Egypt. The people in Jesus' day constructed booths to live in for the duration of the week-long festival to recall the blessings of God.

In the normal course of events, Jesus would have gone to Jerusalem for this feast, but he knows of the danger that the holy city holds for him at this time. His own family members sarcastically chide Jesus, urging him to go and display his power. It may be that they do not take the threat seriously; they certainly do not take Jesus seriously. Though they demonstrate no faith at this stage, at least one of Jesus' brothers, James, did eventually believe; he later became the leader of the church in Jerusalem (ACTS 12:17, 15:13; GAL. 1:19).

In telling his brothers that he was not going, Jesus may be implying that he is not yet ready to go and that, when he does go, he would not go in the way they expected. The expectation of a Messiah included the hope of an immediate deliverance from all national foes and the institution of a sovereign Israel to rule the world. In that sense, the time for Jesus' coming to Jerusalem has not come even to this day.

The religious leaders, however, tolerate no threat to their authority. What is implied in verse 13 will become clear in chapter 9—acclaiming Jesus as the Messiah would result in rejection by the community.

Blind man given sight — they threw him out!

Consider:

3. *This conversation between Jesus and his relatives suggests that things were not easy for Jesus at home. What do you think created a barrier between Jesus and his brothers? How does Jesus' turbulent family life help you through rough times in your most intimate relationships?*

4. *When have you ever lived in circumstances in which others did not take your Christian faith seriously? What problems did this create? How did you handle them?*

John 7:14-52

In this gospel, those who challenged Jesus throughout his ministry, are called "the Jews." Many Jewish people did believe, so this term cannot include all the Jews. Quite probably it referred to the most learned in the Jewish laws and traditions who preferred to try attaining righteousness through a rigorous obedience to the letter of the law. Certainly many of the priests, scribes and Pharisees were included in this group, as the synoptic gospels point out (MT. 16:12; MK. 14:10; LK. 20:19-20).

Jesus indicates that a person must do God's will first to know whether or not his authority came from God. This was hardly a satisfying answer for those who demanded tangible proof, but it again underscored the vital necessity of belief as a basis for a relationship with Jesus. Augustine later agreed when he declared that understanding was the reward for faith, not the basis for it.

One obstacle to such belief lies in Jesus' apparent disregard for the authority of the law as interpreted by the Jewish leaders. Verses 21-24 refer to Jesus' healing of the lame man on the Sabbath (5:1-15), an action that flagrantly ignored the pharisaical values.

Yet Jesus' response brings to light the absurdity of their rules. Obviously, some laws override others—the law of circumcision took precedence over the law of keeping the Sabbath. In the same way, Jesus' work of restoration, a law of the new kingdom that Jesus brought (3:15), had a higher priority.

Another of the issues that became a stumbling block was the fact that Jesus came from Nazareth in Galilee (1:45, 7:27, 41, 52). At least two traditions concerning the Messiah's origin were commonly proposed: one that he would be a mysterious person of unknown origin (7:27); and another that he would come from Bethlehem, the City of David (7:41-42, 52; JER. 28:5; MT. 2:4-6; MIC. 5:2). Either way, a Galilean (from northern Palestine) Messiah does not fit. Apparently, it was not common knowledge that Jesus was born in Bethlehem (MT. 2:1; LK. 2:1-7).

Jesus' response (7:28-29) indicates that it was his heavenly origin that validated his teaching. For those who have chosen disbelief, knowing his birthplace would have no power to persuade.

Between the recorded debates about his identity (7:25-32, 40-52), Jesus briefly introduces his death, resurrection, and ascension (7:33-34). Again, the disbelief of the Jews causes them to misinterpret this reference. They conclude that he must be planning to spread his teachings among those Jews who were dispersed throughout the Greek world outside of Palestine.

Jesus waited until the closing ceremonies of the feast to make his strongest claims. During these festivities a priest would pour water on the altar, offering God thanks and praise for the gift of water that enables the harvest and for the provision of water in the wilderness (Ex. 17:22-27; I Cor. 10:1-4).

To the Jew, Jesus' words may have echoed the words of God in Isaiah, "Ho, every one who thirsts, come to the waters...incline your ear, and come to me; listen, so that you may live" (Is. 55:1, 3). Water had become symbolic of God's abundant provision for both the physical and spiritual needs of God's people (Is. 12:3).

Verse 39 is evidently John's post-Pentecost editorial comment. He understands that the ministry of Jesus continued after the ascension through the power of the Holy Spirit.

5. Some argue that it seems unreasonable to insist on belief in Jesus before having the assurance that Jesus' claims are true (7:17). How far do you think reason can take us in the search for eternal truth? Why?

6. Why do you think Jesus did not tell those who questioned him that he was born in Bethlehem? Why did they think it important that the Messiah fit the clues given in the Old Testament? How is it important to know that Jesus "fits" with Old Testament prophecy?

John 7:53— 8:11

The scribes and Pharisees, in bringing to Jesus the woman who had been caught in the act of adultery, hope to trap him and thereby discredit his teachings in the eyes of the people. They remind him of the law of Moses that adulterers should be put to death (Lev. 20:10; Dt. 22:22). (The law, however, said that both the man and the woman involved in adultery were to be executed. The scribes and Pharisees conveniently overlook the man's responsibility; only the woman suffers the disgrace of public exposure of her sin.)

Although the Mosaic law still stood, under the Roman administration of Palestine the Jews had no authority to condemn anyone to death. If Jesus supports the Mosaic death penalty, he could be accused of interfering with Roman rule. If, on the other hand, he advises that the woman receive mercy, he would appear to condone her sin and could be accused before the common people of not respecting their sacred laws.

What did he write on the ground? We cannot know if he actually wrote words or not, but there are some interesting possibilities proposed by scholars:

- He may have been writing the names of women with whom some of the scribes and Pharisees themselves had had adulterous relationships, thereby silently accusing them of equal guilt.

- He may have been listing other sins of which anyone could be guilty, like greed, lust, hatred, etc.

- He may have been simply doodling to give himself time to think and pray or to wait for the accusations against the woman to stop.

- He may have been writing the first few words of the Mosaic law to which the scribes and Pharisees were referring, indicating that the man involved in the adultery was equally condemned under the law.

In any case, the accusers got the message and crept away.

In his deep compassion Jesus did nothing to humiliate further the terrified woman. He said, "Neither do I condemn you," echoing a theme mentioned earlier in 3:17, "Indeed, God did not send the Son into the world to condemn the world…"

7. The so called "double standard," where women are condemned for sexual sins and men are not, was in effect in Jesus' day. What examples of the double standard can you see in our society? Can you think of any instances besides sexual encounters where the double standard is applied? Is it in effect where you work? in your home? How are both judgment and mercy above such prejudices?

8. Why is it important that Jesus did not come into the world to condemn us? What in our own lives condemns us? What is the Christian "cure" for the feeling of condemnation? How is Jesus' reprieve linked to his command to "go...and do not sin again"?

3/30/08

John 8:12-30

Jesus introduces another discourse that further supports his identity. Jesus begins with the second of his "I am" statements, which recalls and builds on the theme first introduced in 1:4-5. Light, in the Old Testament, symbolized God's presence (Ps. 4:6); Jesus claimed to incarnate that light (Heb. 1:3)—a claim that the Pharisees proceeded to discount based on a lack of witnesses.

Jewish law demanded at least two witnesses in order to substantiate a claim (Dt. 19:15). Jesus offers those two witnesses in himself and the Father (8:17-18). Clearly this would not satisfy one who chose not to believe. Truth is its own testimony, but not even truth can convince someone whose mind is already made up.

Again, Jesus aligns himself implicitly with the Father; the statement in 8:19 is voiced again and again in the gospel (14:6, 9, 17:3)—by knowing, loving and believing in this Jesus, we can know, love and believe in God. The passage contains references to Jesus' death and resurrection (8:21, 28); these teachings fall on blind hearts (8:22) as well as believing ones (8:30).

Consider:

9. *As you follow Jesus, in what ways do you see him as the light of the world? as the light of your life? In your experience, what makes truth hard to determine when material proof is not available? Why is some skepticism healthy? Why is faith also a healthy thing? Name several things, outside of the area of religion, that we accept by faith.*

10. *What do you think Jesus meant by the phrase "die in your sins" (8:24)? What is the alternative he was offering?*

John 8:31-59

Apparently some Jews had heard Jesus' words and had professed faith for a time, but now they no longer believed. Jesus confronted these former believers with the call to cling to his teaching and thereby know the truth, for the truth would make them free. Yet these Jews rejected the need for freedom.

Their resistance to Jesus' words about slavery shows a blatant refusal to accept truth. The descendants of Abraham had been among the most enslaved people in history. Early on, they had spent some four hundred years as slaves in Egypt. Later, the ten northern tribes were carried off by the Assyrians. Later still, the southern kingdom went into captivity in Babylon. And even after they returned to their own lands, this southern group remained subjects of the Persians.

In subsequent years, the children of Abraham were successively dominated by the Greeks, the Ptolemy dynasty of Egypt, the Selucids and following a brief period of independence, the Roman Empire, which subjugated Israel in Jesus' day. Thus, when these Jews said to Jesus, "We...have never been slaves to anyone," they were demonstrating not simply a misunderstanding of Jesus' words, but an obstinate blindness to the reality of their situation.

Jesus did not comment on the obvious nonsense of their defense but cut to the heart of the matter. In referring to their slavery to sin, Jesus confronts the self-deception that had enabled the people to overlook their bondage to sinful attitudes and practices. Such behavior demonstrated their spiritual heritage.

The Jews had boasted in their heritage, for they were descendants of Abraham, a man blessed by God. Yet Jesus said that true children of Abraham would behave like Abraham (8:39) by welcoming a messenger from God. Yet in refusing to be persuaded by truth and in trying to silence truth by killing Jesus, they behaved like children of the devil, who was the opposite of truth.

Here again John expounds on a theme first introduced in the prologue (1:14, 17). The word *truth* in several different forms, appears 13 times in this passage (8:13-58). This repetition drives home Jesus' message about his identity, his mission and his universal offer. Yet Jesus insists that the inability to hear (and receive) his message is rooted in an unwillingness to belong to God (10:26).

By calling Jesus a Samaritan, the Jews disown him; by accusing of demon-possession, they hope to create doubts about his sanity. They press on in their comparison of Jesus with their ancestor Abraham, yet Jesus far surpasses the venerable father of the Jewish race. He makes that clear with an awesome claim—"before Abraham was, I am!" This is more than a claim to pre-existence; he appropriates the conventional name of God for himself (Ex. 3:14), thus provoking the angry Jews to impose the death penalty for blasphemy (Lev. 24:16).

Consider:

11. *The Jews were expressing delusion and denial when confronting Jesus with their own history. In what ways do people today use delusion and denial in their personal relationships? in dealing with family members? in eating habits? in hearing criticism about themselves?*

12. *What does your behavior reveal about your spiritual parentage (8:41)? How do you think Jesus' words about spiritual parentage relate to his conversation with Nicodemus (3:1-15)? (Also see 1:12-15.)*

13. What does Jesus' offer of freedom mean to you? To what degree are you aware of being free from sin? In what sense is knowing the truth and being freed a process?

14. What impact did Jesus' identification with God as Father have on the Jews? on you?

Group Activities

1. Make available construction paper, tissue paper and rubber cement. Invite group members to illustrate in a torn paper collage the dichotomy Jesus expresses in 8:23. Allow time for volunteers to explain their collages; then discuss:

   • How is Jesus like us? How is Jesus unlike us?

   • Are we no longer of this world in the same sense that Jesus was not of this world? Why or why not? (See 17:14-16.)

2. Record each of the following references on a 3" x 5" card:

Psalm 1:3	John 4:10
Psalm 42:1	Isaiah 44:3
Isaiah 12:3	Revelation 21:6
Revelation 7:17	Revelation 22:1-2, 17

   Divide into groups of two or three and give each group a card and a pen or pencil. Ask the groups to read the verse(s) listed and to discuss:

   • What does water symbolize in this passage?

   • In what ways does our community experience the fullness of that symbol?

3. Invite group members to complete the following as many times as possible:

   • The truth has set us free to...

   Record brainstorming ideas on chalkboard or newsprint.

4. Invite group members to roleplay the conflict between Jesus and the disbelieving Jews. Suggest that they put the roleplay in a contemporary setting. What words might Jesus use today to declare his identify? What objections do unbelievers today have to Jesus' claims?

Journal Meditation

The conflict between Jesus' call and the religious leaders' preconceptions about who he really was has been a major theme in this study. The leaders discounted that fresh call from God in Jesus and retreated behind the safe walls of education, religious tradition and spiritual heritage.

Consider your own assumptions about your relationship with God and how Jesus fits into that relationship. What does Jesus say in these two chapters that challenges those assumptions? How is Jesus' call stretching you beyond your safe walls? In what ways do you take refuge in your traditions or spiritual heritage? Record your thoughts in the space below.

Stepstone to Prayer

Lord, may your words find a place in my heart.

John 9–10
The Testimony of Jesus' Works

THE KEY TO UNDERSTANDING THESE TWO CHAPTERS lies in Jesus' words in 10:38: "...even though you do not believe me, believe the works..." John calls on Jesus' great works as further evidence of his identity.

Chapter 9 records the healing of a man born blind, vividly illustrating Jesus' claim first made in 8:12 and repeated in 9:5: "I am the light of the world. Whoever follows me will never walk in darkness but will have the light of life."

Chapter 10 contains the beautiful and beloved teaching of the Good Shepherd and introduces two more "I am" statements that reveal Jesus' mission. The chapter closes with another confrontation between Jesus and unbelieving Jews who reject him as a blasphemous troublemaker. Read JOHN 9–10.

Find the Facts

Who assumed that sin was the cause of the man's blindness? On what day of the week did Jesus heal the man? How did the healed man identify Jesus when the man was first questioned by the Pharisees? What was the season of the year when Jesus attended the Feast of the Dedication? Identify the two "I am" statements in chapter 10.

1. *What intermediate steps in faith did the healed man in chapter 9 go through before he believed that Jesus was the Messiah? Why do you think these intermediate steps were necessary? What were the steps in faith you made before you came to your present understanding of who Jesus is?*

2. *What two images did Jesus use in chapter 10 to explain his relationship to those who sought God? What modern equivalents for these two images can you suggest? Explain the reasons for your suggestions.*

John 9:1-12

John devotes an entire chapter to this one healing story; we can assume therefore that John considered it important. One of the introductory statements that John made was that Jesus is light in the world's darkness (1:4-5). The healing of the man born blind offers literal evidence of darkness being changed to light.

Note that Jesus' disciples, on first seeing the blind man, assume that sin caused the blindness. In that day, many believed that any affliction revealed divine punishment for a specific sin. Such sin could even have been committed in the mother's womb by the individual's soul, or it could be a sin committed by the parents (Ex. 20:5).

Though sin was considered an individual's action that had far-reaching, communal ramifications, the prophet Ezekiel communicated God's displeasure with the blanket condemnation imposed on the children of the unrighteous (EZEK. 18:1-3). "A child shall not suffer for the iniquity of a parent, nor a parent suffer for the iniquity of a child; the righteousness of the righteous shall be his own, and the wickedness of the wicked shall be his own" (EZEK. 18:20).

Jesus goes a step further and rejects completely any certain cause/effect relationship between a particular sin and suffering, though elsewhere he does teach that there is a connection between unrepentance and judgment (LK. 13:1-5).

Though he goes on to explain the outcome of this man's affliction, he does not explain its cause, nor does he generalize about the reason people suffer. This man's blindness presented an opportunity to display the "works of God" and John calls this to his reader's attention as another witness to inspire belief.

Consider:

3. *In what ways does the tendency to link suffering to sin show up today? What are the problems with making such a connection? In what sense is the sinfulness of all humanity the source of many afflictions?*

4. *Are there any ways in which children do suffer for the sins of their parents? Give some specific examples.*

John 9:13-34

This section records two rounds of questioning directed at the healed man. The Pharisees look for charges to use against Jesus and hope this man will provide them with "ammunition."

In this whole incident, the healed man appears as a steady, common sense kind of man, a likeable individual. Notice the manner in which he answers the questions put to him. First, he gives an unadorned, straightforward account of the healing miracle itself (9:15). Next, when asked his opinion of Jesus, he gives a conservative answer to the effect that, if nothing else, Jesus is a prophet (9:17).

Later, when the Pharisees seek to make the man call Jesus a sinner, this grateful, healed man gives a down-to-earth reply: "One thing I do know, that though I was blind, now I see" (9:25). Again, when the Pharisees try to make him rehash the whole story, he points out that he has already answered their questions. He even chides them, asking the Pharisees if they wish to become Jesus' disciples (9:27). Finally, when the Pharisees brand Jesus as a sinner, this solid, ordinary man points out how illogical their charge is (9:30-33).

When the healed man's parents are questioned, they refer the matter to their son, saying "Ask him, he is of age." Their meaning is that their son is of the age to be a legally acceptable witness in his own right. For John, too, this man is an excellent witness to the messiahship of Jesus Christ because he refuses to be rattled by aggressive questioning. He gives plain, forthright answers. He does not try to dazzle anyone with fancy words. He simply points to the evidence: "I was blind. Now I see."

5. When the Pharisees fail to persuade the healed man to say anything against Jesus, they label the man as one "born entirely in sin" and cast him out (9:34). What labels do we sometimes use today to dismiss from consideration someone we do not wish to take seriously? How do labels sometimes blind us to a person's worth as a child of God? What labels do some people use to diminish Jesus' worth?

6. What methods did the Pharisees use to discredit the miracle? What forms does our skepticism sometimes take when we discount the miraculous around us?

John 9:35-41

There is a wonderful turnaround in this passage. Because of belief, the man born blind comes to "see," while the Pharisees, who were born with their eyesight, are "blind" to the truth. Thus, Jesus gives the blind man sight on two levels, the physical and the spiritual.

Earlier, when challenged by the Pharisees, this man calls Jesus a prophet (9:17). Now the man accepts Jesus as the Son of man, another title for the promised Messiah. When this clear-thinking man recognizes Jesus as the Christ, it is a powerful testimony in support of John's claims about Jesus. Once the man accepts Jesus for who he is, he worships the Christ.

Jesus then makes a general comment about judgment being the reason he came into the world. John has already stated that Jesus did not come to condemn (3:17), so the two words ought not to be used interchangeably.

Judgment refers to a forced decision. Whenever Jesus confronts people with the truth, they are forced to make a choice about him. Are they to believe him or not? If not, then the consequences of rejecting him become their own judgment, resulting in condemnation (3:18).

Judgment is also tied to John's use of the word *light*. The light Jesus cast shows things for what they really are. Judgment does the same—it shows unbelief, hatred, jealousy and the like for what they really are. In God's light, they can no longer be called honest skepticism, self-fulfillment or love.

Consider:

7. *What things kept the Pharisees from "seeing"? What things keep us from seeing? What kind of healing do you need in order to share the healed man's faith (9:38)?*

8. *Do you think the healed man was primarily convinced about Jesus' identity because of the healing miracle or because of the personality of Jesus? Why? Is there anything in your own experience that causes you to select the answer you did? Explain.*

9. *What was the price of gaining spiritual sight for the blind man? What price have you had to pay for spiritual sight?*

10. *Compare Jesus' interaction with the blind man to his ministry to others up to this point in the gospel (Nathanael, 1:43-51; Nicodemus, 3:1-15; Samaritan woman, 4:1-26; lame man, 5:1-5). How are they similar? dissimilar? What does this story add to John's testimony to Jesus?*

April 6th

John 10:1-21

Jesus introduces the third and fourth "I am" statements through this figure, or word picture that conveys a truth. These two "I am" statements more directly concern Jesus' relationship with those who accept his invitation to follow him. For them he is the gate for the sheep (10:7) and the good shepherd (10:14).

On one level, these two images are interchangeable, for in the normal practice of sheepherding the shepherd would lead the sheep into a walled enclosure. Often these enclosures, or "folds," had no door or gate. The shepherd would lie down across the opening through which the sheep entered, thereby becoming the door himself. The sheep could not wander off, and no marauding animal could enter, without waking the shepherd.

Elsewhere Jesus makes clear that he himself serves as the entryway into God's kingdom (14:6). In this sense, the image of a door adds a unique dimension to the revelation of Jesus to the world. To find security and well-being in the fold, the sheep must be willing to pass through the door.

Jesus is also our good shepherd. This image generated a great deal of controversy (10:19, 33), for the title "shepherd" occasionally referred to kings and religious leaders in the Old Testament (2 SAM. 7:7; Is. 56:10-11). Even more provoking, though, was that God frequently used the shepherd/sheep image to define the relationship between God and God's people (Ps. 23:1; EZEK. 34:1-31).

The word *good* (Gk., *kalos*) implies more than moral strength or virtuous leadership. It includes the idea of excellence, of beauty; good signifies an attractiveness about the shepherd. As the good shepherd, Jesus holds an irresistible appeal for his sheep; they follow him because he is altogether lovely.

What made the shepherd good, however, was not just the character of his leadership, but also his willingness to die for the sheep. His voluntary sacrifice (10:11, 15, 17-18) distinguishes him far above all hired hands, who cared for the sheep only insofar as they benefitted from the responsibility.

Consider:

11. *Who do you think Jesus had in mind when he spoke of "hired hands" in verses 12-13? What kinds of persons might Jesus describe as "hired hands" today? as "good shepherds"? When have you behaved like a hired hand? like a good shepherd?*

12. Verse 16 speaks of "other sheep." Years later, Christians came to understand that this phrase referred to Gentiles, people not of the Jewish fold. John himself is quite clear that Jesus died for everybody and that whoever believes (3:16) will be saved. What is the mission of the Church today regarding those who are not in Jesus' flock? What is our mission regarding those who are fervent believers in a non-Christian religion? Are these people "other sheep" as well? Why or why not?

13. What characteristics of sheep are helpful descriptions of Christians today? What contemporary image might Jesus have chosen today? Why?

John 10:22-42

A time gap appears between verses 21 and 22, for the setting of this passage is the Feast of Dedication, a winter festival known as Hanukkah today. During the period between the Old and New Testaments, a Syrian king by the name of Antiochus IV, captured Jerusalem and desecrated the temple by establishing idol worship there.

Later, the Jews under Judas Maccabeus recaptured the city and cleansed the temple of idolatry. The temple was then rededicated to the exclusive worship of God. Hanukkah commemorates this rededication and the events surrounding it.

The group who challenges Jesus in this passage ask how long he will keep them in suspense. Although Jesus has given many hints about his identity he has only explicitly revealed himself as the Messiah to the Samaritan woman (4:26) and to the man born blind (9:37). To the rest, he provides evidence and waits for them to draw their own faith conclusions.

The unbelief did not stem from any lack of understanding, for his words clearly delineated both his identity (10:30) and his mission (10:9). His works also declare the truth (10:38). Clearly the unbelieving Jews understood the significance of Jesus' claims (10:33); their unbelief proceeded from an inner rejection of the message.

Jesus' response to their judgment reveals a typical Jewish rabbinical argument based on scripture. He defuses their anger by pointing out that even mere man, having been commissioned by "the word of God" as God's deputies, are called "gods" in scripture (Ps. 82:6-7). How much more logical that the one "consecrated" (set apart) and "sent" (on a unique mission), who incarnated the Word of God, could call himself God's Son.

Jesus concludes by again demanding a decision. "Judge me," Jesus says, "by what I do, for my works are the works of my Father" (10:37-38). This invitation reiterates the conclusion reached at the end of chapter 9, in which Jesus' work of restoration declares his identity (9:33).

14. Why do you think Jesus kept returning to Jerusalem for various feasts when the danger was so great? The other gospel writers do not record all of these visits. Why do you think John includes them?

15. What, according to Jesus, is the key to eternal life? What are some ways you listen to Jesus' voice?

16. What works recorded in scripture have most clearly revealed to you Jesus' relationship with the Father? What signs of Jesus' working in your own life most clearly reveal his love and calling?

Group Activities

1. Draw a six-sided sheepfold on a chalkboard or on newsprint. This should be a simple "aerial view," i.e., six lines forming a hexagon. In JOHN 10, Jesus said that the sheep who followed him were in the fold. Ask the group to decide together what six qualities form the boundaries between the fold and rest of the world, and then write these things next to the six sides of the sheepfold.

   For example, such things as "faith in God" or "good works" might be sheepfold walls. Remember that these are to be group decisions. If someone suggests a quality that others do not see as vital to Christianity, then that person should explain his or her choice to the group. However, only those things that the group agree on by consensus should be written on the fold walls.

2. Invite group members to look up in a Bible dictionary the various Jewish festivals mentioned in John: Passover (2:23), Pentecost (5:1), feast of Tabernacles (7:2), Hanukkah (10:22). Ask group members to discuss what similar kinds of observances are part of the Christian tradition. Ask the group how Passover and Pentecost come to have such strong ties to the Christian faith.

3. Invite group members to pair up and provide one blindfold for each pair. Instruct one member of each pair to wear the blindfold and ask the other member of each pair to relate his or her faith journey to the blindfolded partner.

   Then switch the blindfold to the other partner and have the second person relate his or her faith journey to the first.

   When this is completed, ask the participants to describe what they "saw" in the other person's journey as a result of having to make their ears do the work of both sight and hearing.

4. Divide into groups of three or four. Ask group members to read aloud EZEKIEL 34, each individual reading three or four verses until the entire passage is read. Discuss:
   • How is this passage like and unlike John 10?
   • What greater understanding of Jesus' words does this passage give?

Journal Meditation

Jesus sent the man born blind to wash in the pool of Siloam. The man did so and "came back able to see" (9:7). Close your eyes and imagine what it must have been like for this man suddenly to lose his burden of blindness.

What burdens do you need to wash away? Think about them for a few moments and then list them in the space below. In prayer, ask God to wash them away or to give you wisdom and strength to deal with them. Record anything else that comes to you about these burdens as well.

Stepstone To Prayer

"One thing I do know, that though I was blind, now I see." Lord, I now see...

John 11
The Raising of Lazarus

(handwritten: 4/20/08)

(handwritten marginal notes:)
1) turning water to wine (2:1-11)
2) healing the official's son (4:46-54)
3) healing the man by the pool (5:2-14)
4) feeding the 5000 (6:1-14)
5) walking on the sea (6:15-21)
6) restoring sight to man born blind (9:1-7)
7) raising Lazarus from the dead (11:38-44)

JOHN REPORTS SEVEN MIRACLES THAT JESUS PERFORMED, and he offers them as evidence of Jesus' true identity. He has saved the most significant miracle for last. The raising of Lazarus, although but halfway through this gospel, is the last of Jesus' miracles recorded by John.

John began his gospel saying that life was part of the essence of Jesus (1:4) and Jesus himself said, "I came that they may have life..." (10:10). In reporting the story of Jesus' raising Lazarus from the dead, John shows Jesus' power over both the spiritual and the physical aspects of life. Read John 11.

Find the Facts

How did Jesus feel about Martha, Mary and Lazarus? What word did Jesus use in speaking about Lazarus' death? Who was called "the Twin"? Based on the evidence of their words, which of the sisters expressed the greater amount of faith when Jesus finally arrived? What made Jesus weep? Who expressed the idea that "Jesus should die for the nation"?

1. *What two or three verses in this chapter strike you as the most essential to the Christian faith? Explain your choice of verses.*

2. *What information about Jesus the man would we not know if this chapter were missing from John's gospel? What information about Jesus the Son of God would we not know if this chapter were missing?*

John 11:1-19

Mary, Martha and Lazarus have not been previously introduced in this gospel, but John assumes that his readers will not only know of them, but will know of the incident regarding the costly ointment with which Mary anointed Jesus' feet. John refers to this as a known fact here in 11:2, but does not himself report the incident until 12:3.

Note that the message the sisters sent to Jesus contained no request for help; it simply informed Jesus of the problem. It would appear that Martha and Mary were confident that Jesus' love for them and for their brother would suffice to bring him to their aid. In the face of this confidence, Jesus' choice to linger where he was two days longer may seem callous.

Knowing the outcome of the story, we realize that the delay was not as unfeeling as it seemed, but why let Mary and Martha go through the grief of seeing their brother die and then mourn for four days (11:17)? There was, however, a popular belief among the Jews that body and soul were irreversibly separated three days after a person died. Perhaps it was important to the demonstration of Jesus' power over death that Lazarus' earthly life be reinstated after this three day limit.

Jesus states that Lazarus' illness would provide occasion "that the Son of God may be glorified" (11:4, 9:3). It is true that Lazarus' death provides an opportunity for a visible demonstration of the reality of Jesus' teaching about life and death; in that sense, the raising of Lazarus brings glory to God, for Jesus worked in the name of the Father.

In John's gospel, however, the "glorification" of Jesus specifically refers to his being "lifted up" on the cross, being lifted up from the grave and being lifted up into heaven (7:39, 12:16). Jesus does not seek glory just for raising his friend; he knows that for him to journey to Bethany and raise Lazarus will set off a chain of events that will only end on the cross.

Jesus raises Lazarus, which leads to Caiaphas' counsel that Jesus should die (11:51). This counsel, in effect, puts a price on Jesus' head and gives Judas an opportunity to betray Jesus. Then comes the cross. The raising of Lazarus becomes the first step in the final journey to the cross, the glorification of Jesus.

Clearly even the apostles understand the danger for Jesus to go any- where near Jerusalem. (Bethany was but two miles east of Jerusalem.) They become alarmed when Jesus announces his intention to go (11:8) and, when it is certain that Jesus is going with or without them, Thomas speaks up saying, "Let us go also, that we may die with him."

Jesus responds to the disciples' alarm about going to Bethany with a proverb (11:9-10), symbolically explaining that even near Jerusalem, Jesus will still be safe for yet a little longer. The "day" of his work is not yet over. Soon however, the "night" of suffering and trial will come.

3. Sometimes, like Mary and Martha, we tell another person of our need but do not specifically ask for help. What qualities of relationship need to be present before you can expect that person to respond to your need without being asked? What qualities of relationship existed between Jesus and this family in Bethany? What qualities of relationship exist between you and Jesus?

4. Thomas urged his fellow disciples to join him in accompanying Jesus to Jerusalem "to die" with Jesus. Was this fatalism or commitment? What are the differences between the two?

John 11:20-37

Both Martha and Mary blurt out exactly the same words when they see Jesus, though they meet him separately. There is reproach in their words, but there is also an expression of belief—"If you had been here, my brother would not have died."

Still, Martha goes beyond reproach to state her belief that even now Jesus can do something. She is probably not sure what, but *something*. Yet Jesus' promise that Lazarus will rise again (11:23) is only comprehensible to Martha in the context of the general resurrection. She even protests the first clues to Jesus' intention when he commands the stone that sealed the tomb to be removed (11:39).

Her confidence in a future resurrection is itself a sign of faith, for a belief in a life with God after death was not a popular belief in many religious circles. (See Mt. 22:23-33; Mk. 12:18-27; Lk. 20:27-40; Acts 17:32, 23:6-8.) Jesus, however, repeatedly taught on the hope of life at the end of time, as well as the promise of spiritual life now (6:39-40, 44, 54, 8:51, 10:10, 28).

Here this teaching rises to an astonishing level, for in this fifth "I am" statement, Jesus claims that he is himself the hope and the promise. More than a miracle-worker, Jesus is revealed as the very source, the essence of the resurrection and life. Death has no claim on him nor on any who believe in him.

Martha responds to this mind-boggling declaration with a ringing, three-fold affirmation of faith in Jesus: that he is the Messiah, the Son of God and the One promised to come.

Mary's meeting with Jesus goes differently, though she begins with the same words of reproach and belief. Whereas Martha hurried out to meet Jesus when he approached, Mary remains in the house until Jesus calls for her.

Martha seems able to function, to discuss her grief. Mary on the other hand, once she speaks her one sentence, breaks into weeping. Note that Mary falls at Jesus' feet—perhaps collapses is a better term—and Jesus himself is "greatly disturbed in spirit and deeply moved."

Verses 33 and 35 combine to reinforce John's early introduction to the incarnation (1:14). Jesus, the incarnate Word who "was with God and...was God" is also very much a human as we are. We have seen him angry (2:13-17), hungry, tired and thirsty (4:6-8), and now grieved and troubled.

In Greek, the words used to describe Jesus' emotions in this passage (*embrimaomai, tarasso, dakruo*) imply a wide range of feelings. The first, translated as "deeply moved in spirit" connotes a level of anger—anger, perhaps, at the loud wailing set up by the professional mourners that were common then, or anger, perhaps, at the tragic reality of death, which separates us from those we love.

The Raising of Lazarus

Clearly he knows that Lazarus will not be dead for long, yet John goes on to say that Jesus was "greatly disturbed" and even wept. He so identifies with the human sorrow of the situation that he grieves with and for those who suffer.

John clues us into the limited confidence of those around Jesus while preparing us, at the same time, for what Jesus is about to do. The people consider that anyone who can open blind eyes can surely *prevent* death. Yet Jesus transcends their expectations in this last, climactic sign.

Consider:

5. When Jesus said, "I am the resurrection and the life," he was referring to something more than physical resurrection. What does his statement mean?

6. Martha gave a three-fold statement of faith in verse 27. With what statement (three-fold or otherwise) would you express your faith?

7. *What do you think Martha expected when she said to Jesus, "God will give you whatever you ask of him" (11:22)? Why? What kinds of things do you expect from Jesus when you undergo suffering? In what ways has Jesus gone beyond your expectations?*

8. *When have you experienced Jesus' entering into the depth of your feelings? What was your response? How has this experience of closeness with Jesus helped you to bear the sorrows and/or joys of others?*

John 11:38-44

The reference to Lazarus having an "stench because he has been dead four days," reminds the reader of the magnitude of what Jesus does. The gospels contain two other accounts of Jesus' raising someone from the dead. Matthew, Mark and Luke all tell of the raising of Jairus' daughter (MT. 9:18-26; MK. 5:22-43; LK. 8:41-56) and Luke reports the raising of the widow's son at Nain (LK. 7:11-16).

In both of these cases, however, the miracle took place shortly after the death occurred. A skeptic might claim that the person had not actually died, but was in a coma and that Jesus only revived the person. In the case of Lazarus, there was no question. Lazarus really died and really returned to life.

The miracle prepares the reader for Jesus' own resurrection in two ways. First, it affirms his power over death. John sets us up for the ultimate conflict—the contest between life and death, in both the physical and spiritual arenas. Chapter 11 reveals the outcome that Jesus will accomplish: the one who is "the resurrection and the life," and everyone who believes in him, conquers death.

Secondly, by comparison the miracle prepares us for Jesus' resurrection. For truly, the raising of Lazarus and the raising of Jesus vastly differ. Lazarus returns with his old flesh, but he must again one day encounter death. Jesus rose, not to his old life, but to a new life. Jesus' body, though similar, is transformed, and he is no longer bound by the limitations of his former earthly existence (20:19, 26; Lk. 24:31, 36). Life overcomes death.

Consider:

9. *Lazarus' physical decay kept Martha from understanding Jesus' purposes. What physical obstacles have kept you from faith? What "stones" has Jesus rolled away to call you into new life?*

10. *Consider Lazarus' thoughts and feelings on discovering his return to life as he stumbled out of the tomb. What do you imagine were his first words to Jesus?*

John 11:45-57

It appears that people were either persuaded by Jesus—"believed"—or they were totally against him—"went to the Pharisees and told them what he had done." No one remained neutral. On one occasion Jesus himself had said, "Whoever is not with me is against me" (MT. 12:30).

The council that convened was the Sanhedrin, the Jewish high court, which was led by the high priest. The Sanhedrin usually met to determine legal questions relating to both civil and religious law, but this council also served as a kind of senate where problems of concern to the Jewish people were debated. As a result of a debate on an issue, an "official" position, and sometimes a course of action, was decided upon.

In the case of "the Jesus problem," it is decided to brand him as an outlaw and quietly (for fear of those who believed him) to order his arrest (11:57). This makes it necessary for Jesus to conceal his whereabouts (11:54) until he is ready to appear publicly for his final week.

The concern expressed by the Sanhedrin, that Jesus could start a movement that would cause the Romans to crack down on the Jews (11:48), was a legitimate one. Any popular leader who attracted large numbers of the populace concerned the Roman authorities. By and large, Rome tolerated the peculiarities and specialized practices of the various peoples in its empire, as long as those practices remained peaceful. But Rome could ill-afford nationalistic riots and would order its troops to squash any movement that appeared to threaten Rome's authority and rule.

Caiaphas seems very pragmatic when he states that it is "expedient" that one man die for the nation. John, however, sees a greater significance in Caiaphas' words, telling his readers that Caiaphas did not know just how prophetic his words would become (11:51-52).

This threat from the Sanhedrin causes Jesus to bring his public ministry to an end. Now, the stage is set for the drama of that final week.

11. *Caiaphas claimed expedience as the rationale for his plan to sacrifice Jesus for the nation. What other motives may have been behind the drive to eliminate Jesus? What moral issues do we as Christians need to examine whenever we consider doing something because of expedience?*

12. *In what ways do we sometimes attempt neutrality about Jesus at work? at home? Why is it not possible to be neutral about Jesus?*

Group Activities

1. List on chalkboard or newsprint the seven miracles that John reports as signs.

   They are:
   - turning water to wine (2:1-11)
   - healing the official's son (4:46-54)
   - healing the man by the pool (5:2-14)
   - feeding the five thousand (6:1-14)
   - walking on the sea (6:15-21)
   - restoring sight to the man born blind (9:1-7)
   - raising Lazarus from the dead (11:38-44)

   Invite the group to discuss:
   - Out of all the miracles that Jesus performed, why do you think John selects these seven and only these seven to report?
   - What progression toward a climax can be seen in these seven miracles?
   - How do these seven miracles support John's claims about Jesus?
   - What does each of these miracles reveal about who Jesus is and how he works in the world?

2. Set up a roleplay using three people to portray Mary, Martha and Jesus. Have Mary and Martha accuse Jesus of not caring enough to come immediately when he received news of Lazarus' illness. Let Jesus say whatever he wishes in his own defense. Incidentally, these three roles do not have to be played by two women and a man. Any three persons can portray them, for the issues involved will be the same.

   Now invite two or more individuals to confront Jesus in an imaginary, but contemporary, setting. Brainstorm different problems that Jesus has not seemed to solve in the manner group members' would expect. Rotate the role of Jesus within the group.

3. Divide into groups of three or four. Give each group a large sheet of newsprint and several colored markers. Instruct group members to work together to produce a drawing that symbolizes Jesus' words, "I am the resurrection and the life." When this is completed, invite each group to share the thoughts behind its members' drawing with the large group.

Journal Meditation

"Now Jesus loved Martha and her sister and Lazarus" (11:5). *Love* is a relationship word. Take a few moments to meditate on the following relationship words. As you do so, allow yourself to recall the memories and feelings that bring these words alive for you.

love	loneliness	teamwork
friendship	solitude	faithfulness
commitment	competition	marriage
companionship	divorce	cooperation
intimacy	acquaintance	kin

Now select the word that summons the strongest response and use the space below to draw that relationship as it is today. Use stick figure drawings. If that relationship is painful write a prayer asking God to heal it. If the relationship is one that brings joy, write a prayer thanking God for it.

Now illustrate the word that best describes your relationship with God. Why did you choose that word? Also illustrate your relationship with God:

- the way you would like it to be
- the way you think God sees it
- the way you think God would like it to be

Stepstone to Prayer

"I am the resurrection and the life." O Lord, the part
of my existence that needs resurrection is...

John 12–13
The Time to Be Glorified

WITH CHAPTER 12, JOHN BEGINS THE STORY of Jesus' last week. Judas Iscariot and the foreshadow of betrayal lurk in the background of these chapters. Unlike the other three gospels, John's account of holy week concentrates much more on what Jesus said during those days than on what he did. However, three notable actions are included—Jesus' anointing by Mary, the triumphal entry into Jerusalem and the washing of the disciples' feet—that define the nature of Jesus' kingship. Read JOHN 12– 13.

Find the Facts

What Old Testament prophet does John mention by name? What group bore witness to Jesus during the triumphal entry? What did some people mistake for thunder? Were any of the authorities convinced that Jesus was the Messiah? What kept them from speaking out? How is the disciple who was lying close to Jesus' breast identified? What was the new commandment that Jesus gave?

1. *What two or three themes appear in Jesus' teaching in 12:20-36 and 44-50 that have also appeared earlier in John? What new aspects to these themes does Jesus introduce?*

2. *By what titles is Jesus called in these two chapters? Why do you think the title that the disciples used for Jesus most frequently was Lord?*

4/27/08

John 12:1-11

Chapter 12 serves as a transition between Jesus' public ministry (chaps. 2–11) and his final hours with his disciples (chaps. 13–17). John reports three significant events that prepare his readers for the fullness of Jesus' revelation in his passion and his resurrection.

The first of these events features Mary, the sister of Lazarus, and Judas Iscariot. Motivated by love and gratitude, Mary breaks open her prize perfume. Nard, an expensive and fragrant oil, was usually reserved for grand celebrations; here it honors Jesus' burial. Such an oil was commonly poured over the head; Mary kneels before Jesus' feet and lets down her hair. Since an honorable woman kept her hair tied up, Mary demonstrates a humility that transcends cultural pressures.

John subtly compares Mary's selfless love with Judas' self-seeking denunciation of her act. His objection sounds good—the perfume is worth three hundred denarii, nearly a year's wages for a laborer. Surely Jesus would prefer that the poor benefit from such a gift rather than have it lavished on him.

Judas' protest, however, only covered his own greed. Many groups that accompanied a traveling rabbi would have a common coffer to which everyone would contribute. Judas, who was apparently considered trustworthy, pilfered the purse.

Yet Jesus does not address Judas' intentions but his professed concern. In essence, Mary acts in worship, and Jesus accepts that worship as a worthy reason for such extravagance.

Consider:

3. *What is your most precious possession? If Jesus were to dine in your home, what feelings might motivate giving that possession to Jesus?*

4. *What does Mary's act say about who she believes Jesus to be? What do you think John intended to communicate by including this story?*

John 12:12-19

Mary's action implicitly introduces Jesus as King, for in the Old Testament kings received an anointing as a sign of God's choice (1 Sam. 10:1, 16:3, 13, 1 Kg. 1:39). The account of the triumphal entry explicitly proclaims Jesus' royal identity, for the waving of the palm branches typically signified the arrival of a victorious king returning to his adoring people after a battle.

The people greet Jesus with shouts of "Hosanna!" This Hebrew word originated as a cry to God for help; by Jesus' time the expression was a cry of praise and worship for God's saving help. A partial quote from Psalm 118:26 is followed by a cry of acclamation uniquely found in John's account (Mt. 21:9; Mk. 11:9-10; Lk. 19:38)— "the King of Israel!" What John quietly introduced in 1:49, he here proclaims throughout Jerusalem.

The entire scene fulfills the prophecy in Zechariah 9:9, though the disciples only understood this in retrospection. Just as that prophecy was fulfilled, the Pharisees unwittingly prophesy about the extent of Jesus' authority—"You see, you can do nothing. Look, the world has gone after him!"

6. *The nature of Jesus' actual kingship would not be understood by the crowds in Jerusalem, for they hoped for a warrior-like national hero. What signs of Jesus' true mission does John give us in this passage?*

7. *Why do you think, after all that Jesus had said and done over the course of his ministry, the disciples failed to understand what was happening?*

John 12:20-36

The preceding section concluded with the Pharisees' statement of worry, "the world has gone after him" (12:19). As if to show the truth of that statement, the next incident John reports is of some Greeks who inquire after Jesus. John understood that the Greeks' request is of greater importance than the content of any conversation they may have had with Jesus, for the Greeks are not mentioned again.

In Jesus' day, the term *Greeks* was often used in a generic sense to mean any non-Jew. "Greeks" in this sense represented the world beyond Palestine. Most likely these particular non-Jews were "God-fearers," Gentiles who worshiped Israel's God but who did not keep the Jewish law (ACTS 10:1-2). By the time John wrote these words, the Church was a reality and had grown well beyond its Jewish origins. By the end of the first century, the majority of Christians were of non-Jewish origin.

When Jesus hears that these Greeks want to see him, he responds with a surprising statement about the hour of his glorification. Evidently this request from Gentiles signaled to Jesus that his mission is completed; only the cross remains. Through his brief parable about the grain of wheat needing to die before it produced fruit (12:24), Jesus tells his disciples that his time had indeed come, his time to die.

Jesus' words become progressively more specific about the centrality of relationship with him. The natural parable in 12:24 leads into a surprising statement in the next verse. If any of his followers' hopes for a national hero are bolstered by Jesus' note of climax and triumph in verse 23, they are probably shaken by these ominous words about relinquishing life in this world. Jesus' words in 12:26 specifically reveal the critical nature of the call to follow and serve him.

Thus Jesus goes on to point out that, though the thought of his impending suffering brings pain, it would be wrong for him to ask the Father to spare him that suffering, for this is Jesus' mission. God's voice from heaven, which disturbs and confuses the crowd, is divine verification that Jesus had correctly read the sign contained in this request from "some Greeks."

Jesus' glorification, closely linked in John's gospel to Jesus' crucifixion, is also related:

- to judgment, for Jesus' death becomes the pivotal point by which humanity receives mercy or condemnation (3:18);

- to victory, for Satan, in his very moment of conquest, is finally defeated (8:44);

- to salvation, for in his crucifixion Jesus is exalted and becomes the focus for humanity's unity and reconciliation to God (3:14-15).

As puzzling as Jesus' statement seems, the crowd around him understands its implications—Jesus' work is almost finished and he intends to depart. The people, who have concluded that, in some sense at least, Jesus is the Messiah, expect such a figure to "remain forever" as the prophets had foretold (Is. 9:7). What Mary's gift (12:3) hints at and what

Jesus' triumphal entry (12:13) proclaims is that Jesus is indeed King. Yet, this third incident in chapter 12 explains the nature of that kingship.

In response to the dismay of the people, Jesus urges them again to decide immediately, while there is yet light, for the darkness will soon overtake them (11:9-10).

Consider:

8. *What was the fruit (12:24) that was produced as a result of Jesus, the grain of wheat, dying? How is that fruit harvested today? In what ways do we die? What fruit do we bear?*

9. *Why do you think Jesus chose to confine his earthly ministry to the Jews, especially since many of them did not accept him as the Messiah?*

10. *In what sense is the world judged by Jesus' crucifixion (12:31-32)? In what sense is the world united by it?*

John 12:37-50

Verses 37-43 contain John's editorial remarks. In view of all that Jesus had said and done, the unbelief was inconceivable. John understands this rejection only in the context of Isaiah's prophecy (Is. 53:1, 6:10). Isaiah understood that God honors the choice of the human heart; those who stubbornly reject God will be further hardened and spiritually blinded (Mt. 13:14-15; Acts 28:26-27).

Though many of the Jewish leaders had accepted Jesus' message, John prepares the reader for the lack of a defense in Jesus' imminent trial (12:42-43). The consequences of open support of Jesus at this critical hour would be religious and social excommunication. Neither Nicodemus nor Joseph of Arimathea, who later buried Jesus (19:38), would raise their voices against those who engineer his death.

In verses 44-50, Jesus summarizes many of the themes that have run through his public discourses. These verses contain the last of Jesus' public teachings and reiterate his teachings on: belief, light and darkness, judgment and salvation, his mission on the Father's behalf, and eternal life. Again, Jesus is the focal point of God's message; everyone who is confronted by Jesus' claims is judged on his or her choice of belief or unbelief.

Consider:

11. *How does the prophecy from Isaiah link turning to God with healing? What do you think this prophecy says about the nature of free will?*

12. *What are the implications of Jesus' statement in 12:45? (Also see 14:7.) How do these statements amplify Jesus' teaching in 12:44-50? Why did Jesus come?*

5/4/08 John 13:1-20

The drama of the Last Supper, as reported by John, centers around the washing of the disciples' feet. John's account of this memorable event contains at least two messages.

First, there is the obvious lesson about *humility* and *service*. Because of the dusty roads in Palestine, sandaled feet quickly became dirty. A good host provided a servant to wash the feet of his guests. Such a chore was undignified and no respectable member of society would demean himself to do it. Even Jewish slaves were excused from this job if a Gentile slave were available. Most of the time, however, in that male-dominated society, the task was performed by women. Thus the disciples are quite astonished when Jesus undertakes the job, and we can understand Peter's protest (13:6).

In washing their feet, Jesus teaches by example (13:15), and sums up the lesson by urging his disciples to do likewise. In Luke's account of the Last Supper, we read of a dispute that arose among the disciples over which of them was to be considered "the greatest" (Lk. 22:24). In that account, Jesus said plainly, "I am among you as one who serves" (Lk. 22:27). It would appear then that the disciples needed this unmistakable object lesson about humility.

Second, this incident relates to baptism. In John's gospel, water symbolizes eternal life (4:13-14, 7:37-38). Here Jesus explains that a spiritual cleansing is a prerequisite of belonging to Jesus. As we might expect, Peter insists on being washed all over. Jesus' reply indicates that the one whose life has been purified, as revealed in the choice to remain with Jesus (6:68-69), needed thereafter only to deal with the small stains of everyday living.

Yet Judas, who was on the verge of betrayal, had held back; he had chosen not to remain with Jesus; he was not clean. Jesus prepares his disciples for this great treachery by quoting PSALM 41:9, thereby indicating that his betrayer would be one who had shared the intimacy of Jesus' fellowship. Even Judas' feet were washed.

In verse 20, Jesus begins to transfer his mission to the disciples. This commission continues throughout Jesus' private teachings in chapters 13–17.

Consider:

13. *What parallels do you see between verse 3 and Jesus' actions in verses 4-5 and 12? Read Philippians 2:5-11. What similarities are there between John's living parable and Paul's hymn?*

14. *In what sense is baptism a "spiritual bath"? What ought we to do about the need for daily cleansing and renewal?*

John 13:21-30

Apparently Judas' behavior had, up to this point, been above reproach with the other disciples' since no one could guess who the betrayer would be (13:22). Even after Jesus' clear indication to Judas (13:26), the disciples misunderstand.

The offer of a dipped morsel was a special sign of honor to the recipient; here Jesus may be making a last plea for Judas' faithfulness—all to no avail, for Judas' departs. For him it is the darkness of rejection; for Jesus it is the darkness of sorrow.

Who was the disciple "whom Jesus loved"? Though never named, he appears again in 19:26, 20:2, 21:7, and 21:20 and is traditionally thought to be John himself.

Consider:

15. What do you imagine were some of Jesus' feelings during this scene? Why do you think Jesus let Judas betray him? What do you imagine were Judas' feelings?

16. What more specific explanations for Judas' betrayal of Jesus can you suggest besides the devil entering his heart?

John 13:31-38

Jesus repeatedly speaks of being glorified. At the time, the disciples assumed he was using the term in the traditional sense, that he would be lifted up in esteem and praise and that his lordship over all would be widely recognized. They also assume that, as his faithful followers, they would be privileged to accompany him on this journey to glory.

In fact, Jesus, speaks of being glorified by being lifted up on the cross (12:32). The glory would be in his act of worshipful obedience to the Father. Thus God would be glorified—the Father's lordship would be recognized by the Son.

Given their assumption about traveling some kind of glory road with Jesus, the disciples are quite confused by his statement that they are soon to be separated (13:33). Peter, always the first to speak, insists that he is ready to lay down his life for Jesus. Only later would Peter understand that Jesus was about to lay down his life for Peter and for the world.

The glue that will hold his disciples together after his departure is his new commandment to love one another, "just as I have loved you." The commandment itself dates from the earliest gift of the law (Lev. 19:18), but Jesus gives it a new supremacy in the lives of his followers. Now the followers of God are not to be characterized by their adherence to a set of rules and rituals, but by their loyalty to and service of one another.

17. In what ways was God glorified by Jesus' obedience? How did the disciples later follow him in that glorification? How do we glorify God today in our home? in our church? in our work place? in our vocabulary?

18. In speaking about loving one another, Jesus was not just speaking of a feeling, but of a choice of the heart. What does it mean to love our friends? people whom we have never met? our enemies?

19. Compare Peter and Judas. In what ways were they similar? dissimilar? What clues does John give us about the ultimate outcome of these two denials?

Group Activities

1. Invite your group to wash one another's feet as an act of Christian humility. Divide your group into pairs and provide enough basins, towels and water for each pair to wash each other's feet. Have men wash men's feet and women wash women's. (If you anticipate that your group might resist this activity, you could ask two group members beforehand to come prepared to wash each other's feet while the rest of the group watches.)

   When the activity is complete, ask your group to complete the following sentences:
   - The part of this activity that made me the most uncomfortable was...
   - The part of this activity that made me most feel a part of this group was...
   - I found it hardest to: a) wash someone else's feet or b) allow my feet to be washed by someone else (select a or b) because...
   - The new thing I have learned about Jesus as a result of this activity is...

2. Ask a group member to come to class prepared to roleplay Judas Iscariot. Use the information in JOHN 12 and 13 to develop Judas' character. Ask Judas to imagine that he is on trial and give him an opportunity to justify his betrayal of Jesus. When the roleplay is over, suggest that the group discuss the question "Did Judas have any choice in betraying Jesus, or was he fore-ordained to do so?" Ask group members to defend their answers.

3. On chalkboard or newsprint, write JOHN 13:34-35: "Just as I have loved you, love one another. By this everyone will know that you are my disciples, if you have love for one another."

   Distribute paper and pens or pencils and ask group members to list situations when they were aware of loving others as Jesus loves. Then distribute three pipe cleaners to each group member. Ask group members to choose one of their situations and, using the pipe cleaners, to symbolize any action, reaction or feeling that they had about loving as Jesus loves. Invite volunteers to explain their symbols. Discuss:
   - In what ways did your experience show to someone else that you are Jesus' disciple?
   - Summarize and list on chalkboard or newsprint the characteristics of loving as Jesus loves.

Journal Meditation

Close your eyes and imagine that Jesus is kneeling before you, wanting to wash your feet. How does his request makes you feel? Decide how you will answer Jesus and then record that answer in the space below. Next try to imagine what Jesus says or does as a result of your answer. Indicate that in the space provided as well.

Now imagine yourself loving as Jesus loves and kneeling before him to wash his feet. Reflect on John the Baptist's words (Mк. 1:7): "The one who is more powerful than I is coming after me; I am not worthy to stoop down and untie the thong of his sandals." What are you thinking and feeling as you wash Jesus' feet?

Stepstone to Prayer

Lord, help me to understand and accept your love
for me so that I may be empowered to love...

John 14
To See God Clearly

5/11/08

CHAPTER 14 OF JOHN'S GOSPEL BEGINS THE HEART of Jesus' farewell discourse to his disciples. This discourse continues through the next three chapters and concludes with chapter 17—Jesus' intimate conversation with the Father.

Chapter 14 is characterized by a spirit of profound peace and comfort as Jesus prepares his disciples for his imminent death and for their work after his departure. Yet the chapter also reveals the disciples' lack of spiritual understanding as three of them express certain concerns of the group. Read JOHN 14.

Find the Facts

Which three disciples are mentioned by name in chapter 14? Where is Jesus going? What is the sixth "I am" statement contained in this chapter? Who loves Jesus? Who specifically has no power over Jesus? What titles or names does Jesus use for the Holy Spirit?

1. *Underline the verse that you think best summarizes the theme of this chapter. Explain your selection.*

2. *Which sections of this chapter do you think were of the most immediate comfort to the disciples? Why? Which sections probably took on greater significance for the disciples after the resurrection? Why?*

John 14:1-7

Moments earlier Jesus told the disciples that he was going away and that they cannot go with him (13:33). This creates not only confusion in the disciple's minds, but anxiety as well. What Jesus said first was not surprising. "Believe in God"—depend on God to see you through and trust God to care for you. But what he said next was powerfully new. "Believe also in me"—rely on me as you do on God; trust me to care for you. No doubt had Jesus' opponents been present, they would again have raised the charge of blasphemy, for Jesus is asking the disciples to think of him in the same way they think of God. "I and the Father are one."

Though the next sentence seems to change the subject, Jesus' words follow directly on the heels of his warnings in 13:33, 36. The disciples shall follow Jesus into his Father's house, heaven, making Jesus' departure not a desertion but a preparation. Jesus promises that there will be room for all when the time comes for the disciples to make this journey themselves, and he goes to ready those rooms.

Though John's gospel seems much more concerned with the present spirituality of those who believe and with Jesus' continuing presence within his disciples (14:23), the promise of a second advent in which the disciples are reunited with Jesus is also strong (21:22).

Jesus has already indicated that he is returning to his Father (14:2) and expects his disciples to know the way there (14:4). Thomas' interruption expresses the confusion of all the disciples and perfectly introduces the sixth "I am" statement of this gospel.

Jesus is the way. By trusting in him the spiritual traveler is on the road to God (1:12).

Jesus is the truth. Jesus incarnates ultimate reality; by walking in his way, the seeker is never deceived (1:17).

Jesus is the life. Jesus' life sustains us on the journey and imparts to us the wholeness that we yearn for as we are ushered into the Father's presence (1:4).

Knowing Jesus implies knowledge of the Father. To see Jesus is to see the fullness of the Father. "No one has ever seen God. It is the only Son, who is close to the Father's heart, who has made him known" (1:18).

Consider:

3. If you had been a disciple present with Jesus in this passage, what effect might Jesus' words have had on your "troubled heart"? Why?

4. In what ways does Jesus come again today? In what ways has he come again to you? What do you imagine his final coming will be like?

5. Is Jesus the only way to God? Is there a way to God for a person who has never heard of Jesus, or who has been raised in another faith that teaches that Jesus is not divine? Based on your study of John's gospel so far, how do you think John would answer these questions?

6. If, in seeing Jesus, we see the Father, what do you think the Father is like?

John 14:8-14

Philip voices an audacious request. In the Old Testament, no one, not Moses or Abraham or any of the prophets, was ever permitted to see God clearly. Moses, who was allowed to glimpse God's "glory" (Ex. 33:17-23), was not allowed to look fully upon God, for as God said, "You cannot see my face; for no one shall see me and live" (Ex. 33:20). Even Jacob, who claimed to have seen God's face (GEN. 32:30), only wrestled with a physical manifestation of God, not all that God is. Even this close encounter with God left Jacob wounded (GEN. 32:25, 31).

Jesus' answer to Philip's bold request told the disciples that what they had seen of the Father in Jesus was all that any human was able to see of God in this life. Jesus is the highest revelation of God (HEB. 1:3). Jesus spoke; Jesus acted. This was all that was to be supplied for evidence. People had to base their faith on what was given, not on the kind of absolute proof Philip was asking for. The gist of Jesus' remark in verse 11 is "Believe me because of what I have *said*, or believe me because of what I have done, but do not expect more evidence than that."

Those who do choose belief will imitate Jesus and will do even greater works. One might argue that no one has done greater works than Jesus, but the *followers* of Jesus, not Jesus himself, took the gospel message to the rest of the world, facing all the ridicule and dangers inherent in such a task.

The promise in 14:13-14 is often taken out of the context of Jesus' teachings in this chapter. It follows immediately on the heels of Jesus' words about continuing his work and relates specifically to the accomplishment of that mission. To ask in Jesus' name is more than attaching his name to the end of any prayer. It implies asking in complete agreement with the whole person represented by that name. Whatever any disciple needs to further Jesus' work will be granted.

Consider:

7. *The first disciples saw Jesus in the flesh, heard his words first-hand and were eye witnesses to his works. Yet, at least for a time, most of them hesitated between belief and unbelief. We have even less evidence than they did, for we have only the record of Jesus' words and works. Is faith easier or harder for us? Why? What other evidence do we have today about Jesus that the disciples did not have?*

8. *What is the purpose of Jesus' granting our requests? What do you think 14:13-14 intimates about Jesus' desire to grant our requests? In what ways have answers to your prayers glorified the Father?*

John 14:15-26

Jesus appeals to the disciples' love for him and teaches that this love is characterized primarily by obedience to Jesus' commands. He continues this theme in verse 21, inserting in the intervening verses an introduction to the Holy Spirit.

Now that the time for Jesus' glorification is at hand, it will soon be time for the Spirit to be given (7:39). The promise of the Spirit, given within the context of Jesus' exhortations to obedience, will enable the disciples to love and obey Jesus.

Jesus identifies this Spirit as "another Advocate" (Gk., *parakletos*), one who stands with someone in need, intercedes on his or her behalf, and gives encouragement and assistance. This Advocate would empower the disciples to be equal to the tasks to which they are called.

Just as Jesus is the truth (1:14, 14:6), so this coming Spirit is truth, continuing Jesus' revelation within them forever. *Another* also defines the nature of this Advocate, for it implies that there is a first Advocate. Jesus first came alongside to stand with all people. The Spirit is an Advocate of the same kind—doing the same works, teaching the same message, loving and comforting and healing.

If the disciples were already confused, this promise of a Advocate no doubt deepened their confusion. Yet the Advocate is intimately linked with Jesus' promise in verse 18. Jesus comes to the disciples after his resurrection in many appearances; Jesus comes again surely at the end of the age. But when the disciples experienced the Holy Spirit, they experienced Jesus' presence in a new yet familiar way.

That presence will guarantee life (14:19) and an intimate communion with God (14:20). The disciples receive that intimacy through love, which Jesus again defines as having and keeping his commandments. Jesus will show his love in return by "revealing" himself, manifesting his love and the Father's love.

Here Judas (also known as Thaddeus, MK. 3:18) interrupts Jesus' teaching with another question. Like the other two interruptions (14:5, 8), this is an expression of honest confusion. Apparently Judas still expects Jesus to make himself and his mission clear to all, exercising his power and authority openly as the Messiah.

But Jesus urges the disciples again to focus on the inner revelation attained through loving and obeying him. Though Jesus does not show himself to the world (14:19), anyone who loves him by keeping his commandments will see Jesus and receive the Father's love. Those who cling to that receive the promise of God's indwelling forever. God does not merely visit, but moves in and remains (14:23; REV. 21:3).

Consider:

9. List the characteristics of the Holy Spirit as given in this passage. Receive (14:17) may also be translated "accept" or "lay hold of." Why is it impossible for the world to accept the Spirit? What characteristics of the Spirit are foreign to the world around us? In what ways have you seen this rejection of the Spirit?

10. Why is it legitimate to define love as an action rather than a feeling? How does loving Jesus help us to see God more clearly? In what ways have you experienced the cause/effect relationship of obedience and the indwelling of God?

11. What are the tasks of the Spirit? What kinds of things does the Spirit teach? What part does "reminding" have in the life of the Church? in your spiritual growth?

12. Read Exodus 25:8 and Zechariah 2:10. What new understanding of God's indwelling does John add to these Old Testament prophecies? What do you think are the effects of having the presence of the Father within?

John 14:27-31

Jesus' parting gift to his disciples is peace, not like the "Have a nice day" kind of peace that humans exchange, but real peace, soul-deep peace. This peace would be essential when the arrest and crucifixion would shake the faith of these followers to their bones.

Though their external circumstances threaten disaster, Jesus reassures the disciples that there is no cause for fear or inner distress. Jesus is preparing to leave them, but even that should be a cause for joy, for Jesus is returning to the One who sent him.

Though "the ruler of this world is coming," though Satan is about to make his greatest play for dominion, he has no real power over Jesus. Jesus' power lies in his obedience, which demonstrates his love; his obedience becomes the banner that all disciples who take up his call to obey may follow.

The final sentence of this chapter, "Rise, let us be on our way," seems out of place when chapter 15 takes up another discourse. But Jesus was not simply saying "Let's go." Rather this last sentence is connected to the remark about Satan, and meant, in effect, "Satan is coming...let us go out and defeat him."

Consider:

13. Jesus understood that external circumstances are often the source of many fears. What comfort does this chapter offer that can alleviate fears? How would you define Jesus' peace? How do you experience that peace?

14. In what sense was Jesus' obedience to his Father a defeat for Satan? In what sense do we defeat Satan through our obedience to Jesus?

Group Activities

1. Lead your group in a study of the Holy Spirit in scripture. Copy each reference below on an index card. Distribute to group members. Have group members read their assigned verses aloud. After each person reads, discuss:

   • What does this verse say about the Holy Spirit? the Spirit's characteristics? the Spirit's work? the Spirit's relationship with God?

GENESIS 1:2	ISAIAH 63:10	ACTS 1:8
NUMBERS 11:25	JOEL 2:28-29	ROMANS 8:11
1 SAMUEL 16:13-14	ZECHARIAH 4:6	ROMANS 8:15-16
NEHEMIAH 9:20	MATTHEW 3:11	2 CORINTHIANS 3:6
PSALM 51:11	LUKE 11:13	1 JOHN 3:24
ISAIAH 61:1-3	JOHN 14:17	REVELATION 22:17

2. Divide into groups of three or four. Give each group one of the statements below. (If you have more than three groups, repeat sentences as necessary.)

   • Jesus is the *way*; therefore we...

   • Jesus is the *truth*; therefore we...

   • Jesus is the *life*; therefore we...

   Ask each small group to discuss the italicized word and complete the sentence in a manner that expresses and synthesizes the thoughts of all group members. Provide paper and a pencil or pen for each group to write its sentence. Then reassemble and ask each small group to read its sentence aloud.

3. When Jesus talked about loving him in terms of obedience, we might immediately think of his new commandment to "love one another." Divide into groups of three or four and give each group paper and pens or pencils. Ask each group to research the following:

   • What other commands has Jesus given in this gospel for his disciples to obey?

   After each group has listed as many of Jesus' commandments as possible, reassemble the group and review the results together. Discuss: How well does our congregation obey these commands? How well do I obey these commands?

Journal Meditation

In 14:12 Jesus promises that anyone who believes in him will do what Jesus has done and will even do greater things. Consider the time that has passed since you first believed in Jesus. In what ways have you done what Jesus did? Have you done any greater works? Record your remembrances in words or pictures in the top half of the space below.

Now consider the time that may be left to you before Jesus comes back to take you to be with him. What works of Jesus do you think he wants you to do? What greater works would you like to do? Draw or record your thoughts in the bottom half of the space below.

Stepstone to Prayer

Lord, reveal yourself—your love, your truth, your peace—to me.

John 15–16
Jesus Has Overcome the World

THESE TWO CHAPTERS CONTAIN THE FINAL SECTIONS of Jesus' farewell discourse to his disciples. The chapters include the illustration of the vine and the branches, warnings about persecution to come, further teaching about the work of the Holy Spirit, and an explanation of what Jesus' departure will mean. By the end of this discourse, the disciples have begun to move slightly beyond the confusion that troubled them in chapter 14. Read JOHN 15–16.

Find the Facts

What is to be done with branches that bear no fruit? What is the seventh "I am" statement? What characterizes Jesus' friends? Why was it to the disciples' advantage for Jesus to go away? How did Jesus answer the question raised by the disciples in 16:17? Why would Jesus not be alone even after the disciples scattered?

1. *What themes appear in these two chapters that have not been previously introduced in John's gospel? Circle any words that have not appeared before or have appeared only rarely up to this point in the gospel. What do these words indicate about the themes of this chapter?*

2. *What words did Jesus use in these two chapters that must have alarmed the disciples? What words offered comfort to them?*

John 15:1-11

Like many things in the realm of the Spirit, the desired relationship between Jesus and his followers is more easily illustrated than explained. Jesus' seventh, final "I am" statement introduces this imagery.

Not only did the disciples understand the image of a vine in its natural setting, they also understood the rich significance it carried from its use in Old Testament writing. The figure of a vine had often been used by the prophets to symbolize Israel and to demonstrate the relationship between Israel and God (Ps. 80:8-16; Jer. 2:21). Isaiah's song of God's vineyard is perhaps the best known and demonstrates God's sorrow over the failure of the vineyard to produce good grapes (Is. 5:1-7). What Israel, as God's servant, was called to be (Is. 49:6), Jesus now is.

As the vine, Jesus is the sole source of nourishment. A branch has no existence apart from its attachment to the vine. Nor does it have a purpose apart from the vine. Nobody grows grape vines merely for ornamental purposes. The *purpose* of a branch is to bear the fruit, but the work of the branch is simply to remain connected with the vine. The vine, in processing the nutrients from the sun, soil and water does all the work and supplies all that the branch needs to bear the fruit.

The fruit-bearing branch is pruned, which makes it even more fruitful. The Greek word used in 15:2, *kathaira*, translated "prunes," has the same stem as the word clean in 15:3.

The promise of answered prayer appears again (15:7), and once again it is tied to doing the work of Jesus (bearing the fruit of the vine) and to the Father's glory (14:13). This fruit-bearing process is the second sign of a follower of Jesus (13:35).

The Father is the gardener who does the pruning and careful tending. The branch need never worry about the gardener's neglect nor the vine's inability to sustain the branches.

The end result of such dependence will be the enjoyment of God's love and the fullness of joy. This joy lacks nothing and is the same joy that Jesus experiences. This joy is completely independent of any circumstances, external or internal, for its source is the communion of love between the Father, Jesus and the individual; this love is sustained by obedience.

Consider:

3. *What meaning does the word abide have for you? How does the image of branch and vine apply to your own relationship with Jesus?*

4. *What is the nourishment that the Christian receives from being attached to Christ? What kind of fruit is God looking for from those who grow from the vine that is Jesus Christ? In what sense have the disciples already been pruned? What other ways do you think the Father prunes us?*

5. *What happens to those branches that are attached to the vine but do not bear fruit? What would keep a branch from bearing fruit? What do you think this passage says about judgment?*

John 15:12-17

Again Jesus sets out his essential command and offers his own life—and death—as the supreme model for that love. Loving like Jesus makes the disciples more than learners or followers; it qualifies them to be Jesus' friends, his beloved companions. The obedience that he asks them to render is not the obedience of coercion, like a servant's, but the obedience of confidence and loyalty.

Though the disciples had indeed chosen to believe in Jesus, their choice only echoed Jesus', for he had personally selected them as his friends (6:70, 13:18). To be chosen repeats the image of pruning. The divine gardener chooses which branches will be pruned and which will be taken away. The gardener carefully determines the needs of the branches and makes fruit-bearing not only possible but certain.

Consider:

6. According to this passage, what is the nature of friendship with Jesus? What specific qualities of friendship does Jesus emphasize? How do you think this kind of friendship applies in human friendships?

7. What is the relationship of fruit-bearing and prayer as suggested by 15:16? How does this compare with your experience in prayer?

John 15:18—16:4a

We can imagine that some unbeliever, hearing Jesus' words, might protest, "Now wait a minute, Jesus. Just because I don't agree with you doesn't mean I hate you." Hate seems like such a strong word, but with Jesus there was no middle ground. We believe or we don't; we are his friend or his enemy; we love him or we hate him.

Just as Jesus is not talking about a feeling when he speaks of love, neither does he speak about a feeling when he uses the word *hatred*. Those who love him keep his commandments (14:15). Those who do not keep them hate him. It is a choice to act out belief or unbelief.

There is in some people, however, a malevolent aspect to this hatred. While in many, this hatred manifests itself in indifference, in others, it is expressed in active persecution. Jesus points out that the disciples can expect to be persecuted just as Jesus had been and would be. The fact that Jesus is innocent of the charges brought against him but is hounded and persecuted anyway led him to quote PSALM 69:4 and PSALM 35:19: "They hated me without a cause."

Verse 16:2 reminds one of Saul, the persecutor, before his conversion. He truly believed he was offering service to God by hunting down Christians. This is why he sought authorization and introductory letters from the high priest before setting off to pursue Christians in Damascus (ACTS 9:1-2). There would be others who were as aggressively active against Christians in the years following Jesus' resurrection.

Jesus indicates that this hatred would be directed at his followers by "the world" because his followers "do not belong to the world." *The world*, as used here, refers to those who choose to live without God, conforming to the society they create. This world becomes increasingly uncomfortable for Jesus' followers as they more and more align themselves with his teachings. They, in fact, become citizens of the kingdom of God, even while living on earth.

Some of the stark either/or, no-middle-ground tone of Jesus' words in this passage is emphasized because of the likelihood that by the time John wrote of these things, the Church was being actively persecuted.

In times of persecution, those who sought middle ground, who tried to accommodate both the demands of the world and the demands of Christianity, were viewed by Christians who stood their ground as traitors, and by persecutors as cowards. It is important in hard times for people to declare boldly where they stand.

There is little doubt that the experiences of the Church in John's day colored their view of Jesus' words as handed down to them. Nonetheless, Jesus clearly confronts those who hear him with a well-defined choice: Believe and have eternal life; refuse to believe and miss the kingdom of God.

Jesus' revelation will be the source of judgment. Before he came, the world had a good excuse; since he has brought God's word (15:22) and done God's work (15:24), their rejection of God proclaims their guilt.

The task of the disciples will be to bear witness to Jesus (15:22), continuing his work. Perhaps this is one of the fruits that Jesus appoints his disciples to bear (15:16). This task will not be accomplished alone, for the Advocate also bears witness and strengthens the disciples' witness.

Consider:

8. *What does Jesus say is the attitude of the world toward the Father? toward Jesus? toward the disciples? In what ways do you see this attitude in the world today?*

9. Some Christians are quite comfortable "in the world" today. Should we be? Why or why not? What does it mean to be citizens of two worlds? Should Jesus' words about "not belonging to the world" ever be interpreted to mean that we should withdraw from the world, as some Christian groups have done? Why or why not?

10. What are the disciples witnesses of? In one sentence summarize what you think their witness would say.

John 16:4b-15

"It is to your advantage that I go away." These words must have greatly disturbed the disciples. They could not see any advantage in being separated from this one whom they loved. The "Advocate," the Holy Spirit, who would not come unless Jesus went away, was only a vague notion to them. How could they imagine replacing the flesh-and-blood Jesus with something as nebulous as a spirit? So Jesus gave more concrete information about the work of the Holy Spirit in order to help the disciples grasp the reality of this Advocate who was to come.

According to Jesus, the Holy Spirit would do five things:

- The Spirit convinces the world of sin (16:8). While the Spirit is the advocate/defense attorney for believers, the Spirit is the prosecuting attorney for unbelievers. This was a turnabout. The world had accused Jesus and his followers of sin. The Spirit rises to their defense by showing where the guilt really lies.

- The Spirit would convince the world of righteousness (16:8). The Spirit opens people's minds to enable them to perceive that Jesus is in the right, that his words are true.

- The Spirit convinces the world of *judgment* (16:8). Evil is unable to defeat Jesus, to keep him in the grave. As a result, the Spirit is able to persuade people that since Jesus is the victor, judgment on all that is not surrendered to him will be real.

- The Spirit *guides believers to know the truth* about what is to come (16:13). This is not so much the ability to foresee the future as to be able to understand the meaning of events as they happen.

- The Spirit *glorifies Jesus* and delivers to believers that which Jesus wants them to know (16:14). Verses 14 and 15 together show how the Father, Son and Holy Spirit are intertwined. The three persons of the Trinity all work with that which belongs to the Father: "All that the Father has is mine. [The Holy Spirit] will take what is mine and declare it to you."

In order to describe to the disciples the continuing experience of God's intimate presence with them, as distinct from Jesus' physical presence and from God's transcendent presence as Creator of the world, Jesus uses the terms *Father, Son* and *Spirit*. But to guard against any misunderstanding that he speaks of three distinct gods, he shows in 14 and 15 the cohesive interplay between the three revealed Persons of the one God.

11 Why is it better to have the Spirit's presence than to have Jesus' physical presence? What things has the Spirit declared to the Church that Jesus could not tell the disciples then?

12. Has the Holy Spirit dealt with you in any of the five ways listed above? Which one(s)? What was the result?

John 16:16-33

Again Jesus' words puzzle the disciples. "A little while" indicates both the brevity of the time remaining before his crucifixion, and the equally short time from the crucifixion to the resurrection, when they would see him again. But at the time, crucifixion is unthinkable for the disciples and resurrection not even a consideration.

Of course, John's original readers, coming to this account with a post-Easter perspective, would understand immediately; they knew about both the crucifixion and the resurrection. However, by the time John wrote, Christian expectations for the second coming and the end of the world had become quite strong. For John's readers, these words of Jesus had another meaning as well: The time is short; the end is at hand; be ready.

Notice that Jesus does not offer a clock-time or calendar-time answer to the disciples' question. Instead he gives them the illustration of a woman in labor who, though she suffers, quickly forgets her pains once her child is born. In the same way the disciples must hold fast to the promise of joy that will soon be theirs. Sorrow now will give place to joy later (16:22). Here, Jesus' joy (15:11) is revealed as a lasting joy similar to the whole life span of a person compared to the brief period of labor pains preceding that person's birth.

For John's readers, however, this analogy of the woman in labor also bears a cryptic message about the expected tribulation to come before the final triumph of God. Thus the account can be read on two levels, for the period of tribulation is expected to be the labor pains of a new age.

Again Jesus teaches them to pray. Here prayer is linked with the permanence and completeness of the joy that will be theirs when they understand the resurrection. In joy they will ask and in joy they will receive. In joy they will have direct access to the Father (Eph. 2:18, 3:12), who takes great pleasure in their acceptance of and love for Jesus.

Jesus had spoken again and again to his disciples and to the crowds in "figures of speech," that is, parables, allegories and analogies. Now the time has come to speak less obliquely. "I am leaving the world and am going to the Father." At this, a glimmer of what was to happen burst on the disciples and they said, "Yes, now you are speaking plainly."

But Jesus knows that they do not grasp as much as they think they do, for when the first step is taken to move Jesus toward this rendezvous with the Father—the arrest in Gethsemane—the disciples scatter and flee into hiding.

Jesus closes his words of preparation with a final reassurance. The world is full of trouble and inflicts it upon the believers just as it soon would on Jesus. But even in that dark hour, the disciples must not be disheartened, for the battle is won. Jesus, on the brink of abandonment, torture, ridicule and a lingering execution has peace and good cheer.

12. What is the relationship between prayer and joy? What is the attitude of the Father when we pray? Why do you think many prayers seem to remain unanswered?

13. How did Jesus overcome the world? How, then, should we deal with the troubles of this world? What signs of the world's defeat do you see today?

14. What does the world rejoice in? What is the attitude of the Church toward these things? What does the Church rejoice in? What is the attitude of the world toward these things?

Group Activities

1. Distribute drawing paper and felt markers or crayons. Invite group members to consider quietly the illustration of the gardener, the vine and the branches (15:1-8) in light of their congregation or group. What kind of branches are

they? What kind of fruit are they bearing? What kind of pruning is being done to the branches?

Invite group members to draw the vine and branches that they represent, labeling the fruit and the areas that are being pruned or that they think need to be pruned. Invite volunteers to share their drawings with the rest of the group. Discuss the differences in perspective.

2. Invite group members to imagine that they are being requested to write a group sermon based on JOHN 16:7-15. Record the group's responses to the following questions on a chalkboard or newsprint:

   • What points from the scripture itself do we wish to emphasize?

   • What will we say about the setting and time in which Jesus spoke these words?

   • Which difficult words or phrases will we want to explain?

   • What is the primary message for today in this passage?

   • What modern illustrations can we include to help our congregation to "hear" this message for themselves?

   • How will we conclude this sermon?

   • What do we want our hearers to do as a result of having heard this sermon?

3. JOHN 14–16 has often been used as a source for the development of the doctrine of the Trinity. Divide into small groups of three or four and give each group paper and pens or pencils. Ask each group to review these three chapters and answer the following questions:

   • What common goals and methods do the three Persons of the Trinity share?

   • What different tasks do each of the three Persons of the trinity have?

   • How do they cooperate?

   • According to the text, how are they One God?

4. Divide into small groups of three or four and distribute paper and pens or pencils to each group. Ask group members to read together ISAIAH 5:1-7 and compare it to Jesus' illustration of the vine and branches. How are they similar? How do they differ?

Journal Meditation

The words of Jesus in these two chapters are words of farewell. Try to recall a parting experience from your own life, one in which circumstances forced you to say goodbye to someone you loved. This could be the result of someone moving away or even dying.

Try to recall not only the event, but the feelings associated with it. The purpose of this is not to raise painful memories, but to get in touch with the fabric of leave-taking. How does the memory of that person continue to influence your life today? In what ways did he or she bequeath to you certain strengths that have changed your life?

Compare this recollection with the work of the Spirit as described in 14:26 and 16:13-15. In what ways does Jesus influence your life today through the Spirit? What part does remembrance play in your spiritual development? In what ways has the Spirit declared to you what is Jesus'? Use the space below to record any thoughts that come to you as a result of your meditation.

Stepstone to Prayer

Lord, I am encountering the tribulation of the world... Impart to me your good cheer...

Focus on John

John 17
Jesus and the Father

CHAPTER 17 GIVES US THE LONGEST RECORDED PRAYER of Jesus, presumably prayed aloud and in the presence of the disciples after his final words to them at the last supper. In it Jesus sums up his own last desires, his prayer for his disciples and his hopes for the Church that was to be born out of their ministry.

Find the Facts

How is eternal life defined in this prayer? Who is "the one destined to be lost"? Who does Jesus pray for besides the disciples? What did Jesus ask for himself in this prayer?

Consider:

1. Write one sentence that summarizes Jesus' requests for himself. Write a second sentence that summarizes Jesus' prayer for his disciples. Write a third sentence that summarizes Jesus' prayer for us.

2. *Why do you think Jesus had to pray? If Jesus is the Son of God and therefore a Person of the triune God, why would he need to verbalize what was already in the mind of God?*

John 17:1-5

This prayer has been called the high priestly prayer of Jesus. In the temple sacrificial rituals, the high priest would consecrate, or set apart for God's purposes, the animals offered for sacrifice. These sacrifices, made acceptable to God, would restore the broken fellowship between the people and God. In the same way Jesus consecrates himself as the instrument of salvation for the world. Jesus, however, is both the priest and the sacrifice.

Though these verses are filled with Jesus' prayer for himself, they are focused entirely on Jesus' desire to fulfill the Father's purposes. Both the Father and the Son are glorified in the cross, which the world views as the ultimate defeat.

Yet power over all flesh is given to Jesus; he has authority over the final destiny of all people. His power is not the power of a tyrant, but of a savior; he is authorized to give eternal life. Though he offers this life indiscriminately to all people, only those who believe in him are capable of receiving it.

"Eternal life" typically refers to an unending existence in heaven after death, but here it is defined somewhat cryptically as to "know you the only true God, and Jesus Christ whom you have sent" (17:3). Here "eternal" relates more to a *quality* of life than to the duration of existence.

Focus on John

Nothing in Jesus' statement in any way denies immortality, but he also refers to a present experience of fellowship with God. "Eternal life" is similar to the phrase "kingdom of heaven" (or "kingdom of God"), which appears in the other three gospels. The kingdom, although it is yet to come in all of its fullness (Mᴋ. 9:1) is also "come near" (Mᴋ. 1:15) and has already come (Lᴋ. 11:20).

Eternal life has that same yet-to-come/already-here paradoxical dualism about it. Since, according to verse 3, eternal life is to know Jesus Christ, the disciples already experience it, for they do indeed know and love him.

Consider:

3. *In light of these five verses, how would you describe the relationship between the Father and the Son? How will the Son glorify the Father? How does the Son glorify the Father today? How do we glorify God?*

4. *According to this passage, how is eternal life experienced? What kind of knowledge do you think this requires? In what ways do you enjoy eternal life today?*

John 17:6-19

Jesus' prayer now focuses on the disciples as he affirms the completion of his mission to them. His mission included many things, but it did not include finding disciples. The disciples belonged first to the Father—they were men and women who belonged to God and who recognized Jesus' manifestation as one who came from God.

Now that Jesus prepares to leave his friends, after caring for them like a shepherd for several years, he reminds the Father of what he has done for them:

- Jesus has revealed God's name by teaching the disciples about God's nature. God's name represents the fullness of God's character. Though the depths of God will never be exhausted (Eph. 3:19), the yet undiscovered truths about God will not refute the fullness of Jesus 'revelation (17:6, 26).

- Jesus has given them the words of God. God has a message for all people, and that message has been delivered in Jesus' life and teachings (17:8, 14; Heb. 1:1-2).

- Jesus has kept the disciples, guarding them from evil and helping them to remain faithful (17:12). Judas also witnessed Jesus' work, but his choice destined his fall, as scripture had prophesied (13:18, 17:12; Ps. 41:9).

- Now Jesus prays for the disciples, transferring the responsibility of their care back to the Father (17:11).

5. What do you learn about belonging to God from these verses? In what sense do you think the disciples were the Father's? In what sense did the Father give them to the Son?

6. Reread those verses that mention the name of God. Now read Exodus 3:1-15, looking for the way God's personal name is revealed to God's people. What do you learn from this Old Testament passage about the character of God? How does an understanding of God's name affect your understanding of John 17:6-12?

John 17:13-19

Like Jesus (17:12), the Father would keep the disciples safe by the power of the name (17:11, 15). Since the disciples of Jesus are now children of God, they face hostility from the world (17:14) and from the evil one, Satan (17:15; Lk. 22:31; 1 Pet. 5:8; 1 Jn. 5:19). The power of God's name will protect and enable the disciples, while in the world, to experience a unity among them like that enjoyed by the Father and the Son (17:11). Knowing that, the disciples have access to the full measure of Jesus' joy (17:13).

Finally, the Father will sanctify the disciples, setting them apart as holy servants of God. In keeping with the priestly tone of this prayer, Jesus here uses the language of the temple. To "sanctify" or "consecrate" something meant to cleanse that object and separate it from common use so that it would be fully available for sacred duty.

The disciples are to be sanctified in that they are to be separated from the claims of the world and fully available to the claims of God. In the temple, sanctification was accomplished through water, anointing oil or the blood of sacrifices. Here the sanctifying instrument is the truth of God's word, made effective through Jesus' own consecration as the instrument of God's glory (17:17-19).

Consider:

7. *What do you think is the nature of God's protection? How do we experience it? In what sense is it our choice whether or not we let God be our protective shield against the onslaught of evil?*

8. *In what ways did Jesus "not belong to this world"? In what ways do you not belong to this world? What conflicts arise because of this tension?*

9. *How did the truth of God's word sanctify the disciples? How does the truth of God's word sanctify you? In what ways do you make yourself available for sacred duty?*

John 17:20-26

Jesus now prays for the Church of the future. This Church would be comprised of those who believed as a result of the witness and preaching of the apostles and of those who subsequently believed as these new converts in turn shared the good news with others. He asks that the Church to come might possess a oneness of purpose and faith, like the harmony between Jesus and the Father.

The unity for which Jesus prays is not mere organizational unity. Surely the proliferation of Christian denominations is not, in itself, an affront to the wishes of our Lord. Jesus was, however, praying for unity of heart and mission, for unity of love and commitment. In these areas, infighting among Christians must break Christ's heart. It is still Christ's prayer for us that we may be one as he and the Father are one.

Jesus gives a third sign to the world—the disciples' unity (17:21). By a sacrificial love for one another (13:35), by bearing much fruit (15:8) and by being of one mind and purpose (17:23; PHIL. 2:1-2), the disciples will demonstrate the truth of Jesus.

To enable this unity, Jesus gives his followers his glory. It has become clear that Jesus' glory is revealed most completely in the cross, his supreme act of humility and obedience. The mantle of his submission to the Father's will has now been laid on the shoulders of his disciples. It is not a burden, but a glory and a power that invests us with the strength to emulate his obedience.

In verse 24, Jesus prays that those who follow him will see his glory. Does he mean that he wants all of them to view him on the cross? Probably not, but surely he does want them to catch the vision of perfect obedience to the Father (the obedience that took Jesus to the cross).

Consider:

10. Read again 13:35, 15:8 and 17:21. How might these three Christian objectives cooperate? What two or three things do you consider to be the biggest hindrances to Christian unity today? How can we overcome them?

11. Obedience is not a popular idea today. We may tend to think of obedience as an Old Testament idea, akin to "keeping the rules." How do you explain the fact that Jesus spoke of obedience and keeping commandments as love?

Group Activities

1. Invite group members to study Jesus' teachings on prayer, including what he taught by his example as one who prayed. In addition to JOHN 17, you may find the following scriptures helpful:

MATTHEW 6:5-8	MATTHEW 27:46	LUKE 9:28-36
MATTHEW 7:7-11	MARK 1:35	LUKE 23:46
MATTHEW 14:23	MARK 11:20-25	LUKE 24:30
MATTHEW 26:36-42	LUKE 6:12-13	JOHN 11:41-42

   Divide the scripture readings up among group members and allow enough time for everyone to study assigned passages. Then go around the group circle and invite each person to tell what is revealed about Jesus and prayer from the portion he or she read.

   Together compare Jesus' prayer in JOHN 17 with the Lord's Prayer (MT. 6:9-13; LK. 11:2-4). What common requests do they have? How do they differ? What are the elementary ingredients to prayer?

2. Again and again in this study of John, Jesus speaks of his "glorification." We have come to understand that he was glorified by being "lifted up" on the cross. Distribute and sing together copies of the hymn "When I Survey the Wondrous Cross."

   After the song, ask group members to think carefully about the testimony that is given in each of the verses. Invite any group member who can identify a personal experience that would fit with any specific verse to share that experience with the group. Repeat this invitation until all who have something to share have done so. Conclude by pointing out that our experiences of the power of the cross are examples of how we participate in Jesus' glory.

3. Some have identified these seven elements of prayer: adoration, praise, thanksgiving, penitence, oblation, intercession and petition.

   Ask group members to reread JOHN 17 and see how many prayer elements can be identified in Jesus' prayer. Compose a group prayer that includes all seven elements and that is centered around the joys and pains of the group members today. Write this prayer on chalkboard or newsprint.

Journal Meditation

What kinds of images come to mind when you think about your own prayer life? Imagine that you want to communicate the essence of your prayer life to a person who is deaf and cannot read. What pictures or images would you draw to explain how you feel about your prayers?

Use the space below to draw those images or pictures.

Stepstone to Prayer

Lord, lead me in the ways of your glory and obedience...

John 18–19
The Betrayal, Arrest and Crucifixion of Jesus

THERE IS A SENSE OF RAPID MOVEMENT IN THESE TWO CHAPTERS. The public ministry of Jesus came to an end a few days earlier. Jesus' private time of instruction and prayer with his disciples has also ended. Now, the painful dark valley must be traversed. Read JOHN 18–19.

Find the Facts

What happened to the group who came to arrest Jesus when our Lord said, "I am he"? Who was Malchus's relative? Why did those who arrested Jesus not want to enter the praetorium? Why did they need to bring Jesus to Pilate? Who was Barabbas? What title did Pilate write on the cross? Who took charge of Jesus' body after his death? Why was the garden tomb used?

1. Take a moment to notice the number of action verbs in today's reading. They reinforce the sense of movement and action that took place in a very short time. Which of these action verbs convey to you that Jesus was handled very roughly during this ordeal? Which action verbs convey Jesus' authority?

2. These two chapters provide a good deal of basic information about what happened to Jesus during his final hours. What truths about Jesus, revealed in these last hours, do you think John wanted his readers to remember? Why?

John 18:1-11 *June 22, 2008*

All four gospel writers report Jesus' betrayal and arrest. They all give similar details (Mt. 26:36-56; Mk. 14:32-52; Lk. 22:39-53), but John includes some details that the other writers do not mention:

- Only John tells us that Jesus often met in this garden with his disciples. Though he is aware of Judas's treachery and Judas's familiarity with the garden as a meeting place, Jesus does not take the precaution of going to a secret place.

- Only John mentions the presence of soldiers (probably Roman legionnaires) and of Pharisees. The display of worldly power—both political and religious—is complete. Jesus looks trapped.

- Only John leaves out Judas's identifying kiss. In John's account, Jesus approaches the armed crowd and addresses them first, demanding that they declare their mission.

- Only John records the astonishing detail about the crowd's collapse. Jesus' presence was not one of timidity or fear, but of kingly power.

- Only John records Jesus' intervention on the disciples' behalf. John includes the explanation of this mediation as a fulfillment of Jesus' own words (6:39, 17:12). Though the disciples flee in terror (Mt. 26:56), they are in no danger, for Jesus still protects them.

All four gospel writers report that one of the disciples cut off the ear of the high priest's slave, but only John tells us that the injured man's name is Malchus and that the sword-wielding disciple is Peter.

The differences in John's account lead to the probable conclusion that he had sources of information that were unavailable to Matthew, Mark and Luke, and vice versa. If John had access to the other gospels, then the parts of the story that John chooses to tell give clues about the points he wishes to emphasize.

These unusual details reveal Jesus as a majestic, authoritative figure—one who purposefully goes to a well-known place; one who overwhelms an armed crowd with only a word; one who appears on the offensive instead of the defensive; one who intercedes on behalf of his friends; one who rejects the way of violence. Surely John wants us to understand that Jesus is able to be arrested because he himself permitted it, not because his power has deserted him (18:4).

Naming Peter as the defender who cut off Malchus's ear reveals that, though Peter was soon to deny Jesus, Peter was not short on love for his Master. It shows that Peter was normally courageous and makes his subsequent denial seem all the more tragic.

3. *Identify some of the thoughts and feelings that might have motivated Judas's betrayal. (See Mt. 26:14-16; Mk. 14:10-11; Lk. 22:1-6.) Compare these with the thoughts and feelings that might have motivated Peter's attempt to defend Jesus. What do you think their hopes were? their fears? With whom do you identify most closely in this passage? Why?*

4. *What adjectives would you use to describe Jesus as portrayed in this passage? Why?*

John 18:12-27

Jesus is now taken for examination before Annas. Though John calls Annas "the high priest" (18:19), he has previously told his readers that Caiaphas was the high priest that year (11:49), as indeed he was.

The position of high priest was extremely powerful, both socially and politically. The Roman government exercised a certain amount of control over the man in that position. Though Annas had been the high priest, he was probably not sufficiently agreeable to the purposes of the Roman presence. The Romans removed him from office in A.D. 15.

Such Roman intervention was greatly resented, and Annas evidently retained a certain amount of prestige and power. Caiaphas, being

Annas's son-in-law, no doubt saw nothing good to come out of challenging the older man's position. After Annas finishes his questioning of Jesus, he sends the prisoner to Caiaphas for "official" disposition of the case. Caiaphas merely sends Jesus on to Pilate (18:28).

A unique detail in the account of Peter's denial of Jesus is the mention of another disciple besides Peter who also followed Jesus to the court of the high priest (18:15). This disciple is known to the high priest (18:16) and apparently also to some of the high priest's staff. He is able to arrange for Peter's admission into the courtyard.

This other disciple is traditionally considered to be the apostle John himself. Why John would be known, and apparently favorably, to the high priest is a question with no clear answer. Nonetheless, without him, Peter could not have entered the courtyard.

One of those who accuse Peter of being in the garden when Jesus was arrested is a "relative" of Malchus. This accusation may have hardened Peter's resolve to deny his involvement, for if he were identified as the assailant of this man's relative he might have been physically assaulted on the spot.

Jesus' defense before Annas simply points out that he had previously said in public all that needed to be said. If Annas is determined not to believe Jesus, then for Jesus to repeat his teaching again is a waste of time. Jesus says nothing at all that is aimed at saving himself. The die is cast; there is no going back.

5. Identify some of the thoughts and feelings that might have motivated Peter's three denials. How does Peter's betrayal differ from Judas's? What do you think Peter's behavior communicates about his true love for Jesus?

6. Consider Jesus' trial before the Jewish court as an episode of injustice. Why didn't Jesus "stand up for himself"? What implications might there be for us in his example? Is Jesus' remark in verse 23 a plea for justice or a challenge for the officer to search for the truth himself? Defend your answer.

John 18:28—19:16

Although the crowd that arrests Jesus is only too glad to escort him to Pilate's headquarters, they do not wish to go in for fear of ritual contamination, which would prevent them from eating the Passover meal. (In John, the last supper is not the Passover meal, but a supper the evening before.)

The praetorium consists of the barracks, parade ground and offices of the elite household troops, the Praetorian guard assigned to protect the Roman procurator (governor), Pilate. This headquarters also includes a military prison and Pilate's personal residence. Since Pilate and the soldiers are Gentiles, the risk for Jews of accidentally coming into contact with a ritually unclean object was high. The procedures to become "clean" again took time and could not be completed before the Passover meal would be ready.

The whole reason for bringing Jesus to Pilate at all is summed up in verse 31; the Jews could try their own people, but they had no authority to execute anyone.

It would seem that Pilate could put an end to this whole affair by simply refusing to issue an execution order, but from Pilate's viewpoint the matter is much more complicated. On at least three occasions prior to this day, Pilate had seriously mishandled certain dealings with the Jews. (We know this information from the writing of a Jewish historian named Flavius Josephus, who was born just a few years after Jesus' death.)

According to Josephus, on at least one of these occasions of Pilate's gross mismanagement, a number of Jewish civilians were massacred. In each incident, Pilate had either had to back down before the Jews, or act with force. When he backed down he lost face. When he authorized force and things got out of hand, he received a scathing rebuke from the emperor. Thus in this "Jesus business," Pilate could ill-afford another fiasco. He does not believe that Jesus deserves death, but neither can he afford to brush off the demands of the highly placed Jews who stood before him (19:8).

Given the forces at play, Pilate tries to find a middle ground. First, he tries to make Jesus the customary token prisoner who was normally freed at the Passover, but the crowd demands a common thief instead.

Next, he tries to make Jesus look ridiculous (19:1-3) and has him flogged, perhaps hoping that the mockery would cause the people to think that Jesus is a harmless fool and that the flogging would satisfy their thirst to have Jesus punished. Neither of these actions deters the mob, however, now demanding that Jesus be crucified.

Pilate tries to return the responsibility for Jesus' death to the mob (19:6), telling them to crucify Jesus themselves. This is not to be taken as permission, but as a reminder that they were impotent to act without him.

Finally, Pilate tries to release Jesus (19:12), but the chief priests and the others play their trump card: They accuse Pilate of not being "a friend of the emperor" if he releases Jesus. This was a not-so-subtle threat to make trouble for Pilate before the emperor.

In desperation Pilate asks "Shall I crucify your King?" Their answer, "We have no king but the emperor," was not a statement of political loyalty, but a reminder of the threat to make things hot for Pilate. The procurator gives up and issues the execution edict.

Throughout all of this, Pilate faces and acknowledges Jesus' innocence. Jesus says little on his own behalf and does nothing to influence the wavering Pilate to let him go. Jesus clearly refuses to stop the process now set in motion. He will see it to the end.

Consider:

7. Do you think Pilate was justified in his decision to allow Jesus to die? Why or why not? What do you think he should have done? Is any political leader ever justified in sacrificing a "troublemaker" to keep the peace? Defend your answer.

8. The crowd is concerned about becoming ritually unclean. In what sense does their action in railroading Jesus' death make them unclean? What is the spiritual cure for such uncleanliness?

9. Describe Jesus' kingship. How might it have interfered with Caesar's authority? How might it interfere with worldly authorities today?

John 19:17-42

Before a crucifixion, it was the Roman custom to write the condemned person's crime on a placard that was carried through the streets immediately ahead of the criminal, staggering under the weight of his own cross. In this way, the criminal's charge of guilt was displayed to the people. When the person was finally crucified, the placard was nailed to the cross as well.

When Pilate writes "The King of the Jews," he jabs at the Jews who had forced him into the awkward position of having to decide Jesus' fate. They had accused Jesus of claiming to be the King of the Jews. Pilate states the charge in a way that ridicules the accusers, as if to say, "Look, this pathetic and broken creature is your king. It doesn't say much for you as a people!"

John views the soldiers' casting lots for Jesus' clothing as a fulfillment of PSALM 22:18. Jesus' unbroken bones and pierced side also reveal the foreordained nature of the whole event (Ex. 12:46; Ps. 34:20; ZECH. 12:10).

"The disciple whom he loved" is thought to be John himself, who, as far as we know, was the only one of the twelve to be present at the cross. This may have been easier for John than for the others since, according 18:16, he was known to the high priest and presumably not considered a threat.

This disciple accepts the responsibility to care for Jesus' mother. It is curious that Jesus commits Mary to John, for Jesus had brothers (Mt. 13:55). When an eldest son died and the father was not living (we presume Joseph died before Jesus began his public ministry), the next eldest son would assume the responsibility for his mother.

Here Jesus places a higher value on the new relationship between the children of God than upon the traditional family lines. A new family is created; a new community is formed at the foot of Jesus' cross. Now those who believe are called to relate to one another in a deeper unity and commitment than to family ties.

Jesus often spoke of this new bond in his teaching, as recorded in some of the other gospels. "And pointing to his disciples, he said, 'Here are my mother and my brothers! For whoever does the will of my Father in heaven is my brother and sister and mother'" (Mt. 12:49-50).

The crucifixion took place on the day of Preparation, that is, on the eve of the Passover. The Jews had a law that a dead hanged man should not remain on the tree all night (Dt. 21:22-23). To leave Jesus, or any crucified Jew for that matter, on the cross beyond sunset was considered a defilement, and especially on this day (Friday) because the Jewish Sabbath began at sundown, and even more, this particular Sabbath was Passover. The Jews believed that the exposed bodies of the dead polluted the Sabbath.

Thus the Jews asked that the death of the three on the crosses be hastened by breaking the legs. A person who was crucified suffered from tremendous pressure on his chest, making it almost impossible to breathe. A crucifixion could last several days, as long as the victim could continue to push up on his legs, thereby relieving momentarily the constriction in his chest and allowing him to exhale. By breaking the legs, the soldiers removed the one possibility of prolonging life, greatly hastening death. This procedure is unnecessary in Jesus' case; he is already dead.

The piercing of Jesus' side simply verifies his death. An emission of blood and water indicates that Jesus' heart, and its surrounding sac, is pierced. This is apparently very important to John's testimony. For those who believed that perhaps Jesus was only a divine apparition, this physical detail refuted that possibility.

The two who took Jesus' body for burial are both highly placed Jews, members of the Sanhedrin, the Jewish high council. Joseph was certainly wealthy, and probably Nicodemus was, too. Joseph is clearly identified as a secret disciple and we assume Nicodemus, whom we first met in chapter 3, has also become a believer by this point. Note that while the accusers of Jesus are concerned that they do nothing to render them ceremonially unclean (18:28), these two handled the dead body of Jesus, an action that positively left them ceremonially polluted for a full week.

Consider:

10. In what sense was Pilate's sign, "The King of the Jews," accurate?

11. Why do you think John points out three occasions of the fulfillment of Old Testament prophecies? In what other ways does the text show Jesus' control over these events?

12. What kind of men did Jesus die with? (Also see Mt. 27:38, 44; Lk. 23:32, 39-43.) What significance do you think this has?

13. Joseph and Nicodemus had been secret disciples of Jesus. Why do you think they publicly declared their loyalty now? What are the spiritual problems with being a secret disciple? Are there aspects of our Christian faith that can be kept secret? that should never be kept secret? Why or why not? Explain your answers.

Group Activities

1. The accusers of Jesus were anxious to keep their laws about ceremonial cleanliness and to preserve the sanctity of the Sabbath, but in so doing they missed the spirit of those laws. Yet the laws of God that we receive from the Old Testament are essential to understanding the content of love-motivated Christian behavior.

   Invite group members to read the Ten Commandments (Ex. 20:1-17). Ask group members to think about each of these ten God-given commands and then, for each command, ask the group to answer the following questions:
   - What does this command teach us about what it means to live as a Christian?
   - What is the spirit of the law?
   - Restate the command in a positive form.

   Ask group members to be as specific as possible, using examples from their own lives or from the world around us, in discussing the questions.

2. Often it is easier to respond to the spiritual meanings behind a straightforward account by thinking in concrete ways. Distribute a pipe cleaner to each group member. Invite group members to reflect for a few moments on each word below and bend their pipe cleaners into a shape that expresses their reaction to this word in light of JOHN 18–19. Read each word and allow several minutes for group members to work.

community	king	power	truth
fulfillment	denial	law	love

   Invite volunteers to explain their pipe-cleaner sculptures.

3. Divide into groups of three or four. Give each group paper and a pen or pencil. Ask each group to select a scribe who will record group members ideas. Invite group members to brainstorm the following:
   - What happened spiritually when Jesus died on the cross? (e.g., forgiveness of sins? reconciliation with God?) Explain your answers.

   Reassemble the group and compare answers.

Journal Meditation

Peter loved Jesus, but was apparently overwhelmed by fear and confusion. Consider times in your life when your loyalty to Jesus has been overcome by other feelings created by difficult circumstances around you—fear, confusion, grief, anger, etc. What behavior did your feelings produce? What feelings do you have now as you look back on those dark times of letting Jesus down?

Jesus knew that Peter would deny knowing him. It did not change Jesus' love for or loyalty to Peter. How does this knowledge comfort you as you recall your failures? How does it strengthen you as you face an unknown future?

Record your thoughts and feelings below.

Stepstone to Prayer

Lord, I am so weak, and you are so strong. Help me to cling to you even when I see no light...

John 20–21
The Resurrection and Beyond

THE ROCK MUSICAL *Jesus Christ Superstar* concludes with a bittersweet tune entitled "John Nineteen Forty-One." The story ends with the tomb. Yet without the events of chapters 20 and 21, all of Jesus' claims in the previous chapters become void. The resurrection of Jesus, his final victory over death, justifies our faith in him as the Son of God who lives today. Read JOHN 20–21.

Find the Facts

Who was the first person to enter the tomb on that first Easter? How many angels did Mary Magdalene see? Did Thomas actually touch the nail prints in Jesus' hands and the wound in Jesus' side? Why did John write this gospel? How many disciples went fishing? How many times did Jesus appear to his disciples after the resurrection? How many times did Peter profess his love for Jesus that morning beside the Sea of Tiberias? Is everything that Jesus did in the course of his earthly ministry written down?

Consider:

1. *What things seem to be uppermost in Jesus' mind in the days immediately following the resurrection?*

2. *According to these chapters, what does Jesus do to prepare the disciples for their own ministries in his name?*

John 20:1-18

When Mary Magdalene finds the tomb empty on Sunday morning, she makes the logical assumption that Jesus' body has been moved. Perhaps she fears that Jesus' tormentors continue their persecution even after death.

When Peter and John arrive at the tomb, they notice the empty burial cloths. This causes John to draw a different conclusion than Mary Magdalene had, for one would hardly suppose that someone stealing a body would take the time to unwrap the body first and then use additional time to roll the burial napkin up in a neat bundle (20:7). This other disciple *believed.*

This is additional evidence that this disciple was John, for the entire gospel that bears his name is written from the viewpoint of *belief.* This disciple is the only one whose belief resulted from the empty tomb. For the rest of the disciples, it will take the actual appearance of the risen Lord before belief will be born.

Mary evidently follows Peter and John back to the tomb, for she stands outside the tomb weeping after the two disciples return to their homes. She still assumes that someone has carried Jesus' corpse off. It never occurs to her that the "gardener" before her is the Lord. Only when Jesus speaks her name does recognition dawn.

Mary calls Jesus "Rabbouni." This is simply the Aramaic form of the word *Rabbi*, which, as the scripture tells us, means "Teacher." Aramaic was the common language of Palestine in Jesus' day, the language that Jesus himself spoke.

Apparently, upon seeing Jesus, Mary clung to him in her joy and astonishment. Perhaps Jesus' gentle rebuke is meant to lead Mary into a new understanding of his presence. Jesus was not simply resuscitated like Lazarus; he was resurrected, with a new and different relationship to this world. No longer would his presence be limited by time and space; his ascension would release the Spirit, through whom he could be present in every believer's heart (7:38-39, 14:17, 23).

Jesus' message, entrusted to Mary for all of his disciples, clarifies the sibling relationship believers have with Jesus (GAL. 4:1-7). We share the same Father, which makes Jesus our elder brother. Yet Jesus does not say "I am ascending to *our* Father, to *our* God." He may be making a distinction between his relationship with the Father, which is one of essence, and the disciples' relationship, which is one of adoption and of grace.

3. *Why do you think Jesus chose Mary to witness his first appearance and to be the first bearer of the good news?*

4. *How did Jesus' resurrection make God our Father in a deeper way? What reassurance do you think Jesus was communicating when he told them he was returning to God? What comfort can we find in knowing that the risen Jesus is with the Father?*

John 20:19-29

Sunday evening finds Jesus' disciples huddled together behind locked doors. Though Mary had given the good news, many likely doubted. The danger of being noticed and identified as followers of a man executed as an outlaw seems more real than Mary's tale.

Suddenly Jesus is present. Perhaps the disciples are overwhelmed with shame at their earlier abandonment and expected some reproof. But Jesus' words reassure and comfort the disciples. As he reminds them of their ministry, surely his words calm their fears. Before his death he intended to send them out (17:18), and their weakness did not take him by surprise nor did it change his purpose.

Jesus breathes on them, reminding the reader of John's new genesis theme (1:1). The disciples are now new men and women who have received a fresh breath, a re-creation, from God (GEN. 2:7). In the power of that gift, the disciples are strong to go out and proclaim the good news of forgiveness of sins through Jesus Christ.

Though the power to forgive belongs to God alone (MK. 2:7), the Holy Spirit within the disciples will convince the world of sin, righteousness and judgment (16:8; MT. 16:19, 18:18). Filled with the Spirit, the disciples would be able to discern between false and sincere repentance, the prerequisite for forgiveness. The Church has the grand opportunity to declare forgiveness of sins to penitents.

Thomas' expressed skepticism seems to mark him as the only doubter among the 11, but Matthew (28:17) reports that some of the others also "doubted." In any case, he may well be the disciple with whom we can most easily identify, for we too are asked to believe without concrete proof, and many of us find that difficult.

Thomas represents those throughout the gospel who continued to ask for more signs (4:48, 6:30). Thomas' faith demands its own kind of proof, but John's subtle message is that the good news will be passed on by Jesus' followers and must be accepted by faith. Jesus' blessing on all of us who have never seen the risen Christ reassures his followers that faith will not depend on sight.

Yet Thomas is a hero of faith as well. Though he could not accept his friends' report, he continued to identify with them. In his doubt, Thomas acts in faith and refuses to abandon the fellowship. His steadfast faithfulness to Jesus' followers is rewarded and, in spite of his stubborn words in verse 25, seeing Jesus is enough to elicit a profession of deep faith.

5. According to this passage, what is the relationship of believing and seeing? How is Thomas's statement related to the incident of the healing of the man born blind (9:35-41)?

6. When a priest pronounces absolution today, who is actually doing the forgiving? What specifically is being absolved? What kinds of consequences of sin cannot be removed by absolution?

7. Read Acts 2:12, 22-24, 32-41 and compare that account of the outpouring of the Spirit at Pentecost with the gift of the Spirit described in 20:22-23. What are the similarities? What was the content of the message preached on Pentecost? What did it say about the forgiveness of sins?

John 20:30-31

These two verses feel like the conclusion of this gospel, and we may be a bit surprised to find that another chapter follows. One thing this passage tells us is that Jesus did many more things "not written in this book," and probably not written in the other gospels either. John repeats this idea in 21:25. John's account suggests that Jesus' ministry lasted three years. Surely in that length of time, Jesus said and did far more than could be recorded in a few brief gospels. We would like to know what some of those other things were, but we do not have that privilege. John freely admits that he has been selective in the events and speeches of Jesus that he has included, using as a criterion those which would most help to foster belief: "but these are written so that you may come to believe that Jesus is the Messiah."

We must assume that this same principle of selection was at work in the writing of all four of the gospels. In a sense, the gospel writers served as editors as well as authors. They selected, from the larger body of actual things Jesus said and did, those things that seemed most important to them. These they have preserved for us. We owe the gospel writers a great debt.

Consider:

8. How does this principle of selection help us to understand that the gospels do not contradict, but rather compliment one another? In what ways do you think your study of this gospel has influenced your belief in Jesus and your experience of "life in his name"?

John 21:1-14

Chapter 21 appears as a kind of epilogue to John's gospel, for by the end of chapter 20 the case for belief has been fully developed. Chapter 21 wraps up some loose ends. We can imagine that a first-time reader of John's gospel might come to the end of chapter 20 wondering, "Yes, but what became of Peter after he denied Jesus?" Thus, this epilogue resolves such matters for us.

However, there is something else going on in this chapter as well, something that is not quite so apparent. Jesus tells the fishermen where to cast the net to catch fish. Some do not see this as a miracle, but rather point out that from where Jesus stands, Jesus may be able to view the water from a different angle and see a school of fish that the disciples, who apparently are right on top of it, do not see.

It does not really matter whether this catch was the result of divine intervention or not, for its significance seems to lie in the number of fish hauled in, 153. Did someone actually count the fish? This is possible, of course, but if John's purpose in telling this story is to impress upon his readers that this is an unusually large catch, a round number would have been just as useful.

The society of that day had a far more symbolic understanding of numbers than we do today. Seven and twelve, for example, were considered "complete" numbers, numbers that signified a perfect whole, possibly because of the seven days of the Genesis creation story and the twelve tribes of Israel. The assumption, then, is that 153 has a deeper meaning.

There has been much speculation about the meaning of this number in the centuries that have since come and gone, and some of the suggested answers border on the ridiculous. Probably the most satisfying suggestion was made by Jerome, the fourth-century translator of the Latin Vulgate version of the Bible. He pointed out that in Jesus' day many thought that only 153 species of fish existed. Catching all of these in a net that "was not torn," could be a way of saying that there was room for all the people of the world (the fish) in the Church (the net).

This at least fits with Jesus' call to the disciples to "fish for people" (Mt. 4:19).

When Jesus "took the bread and gave it to them" (21:13), we can imagine that the actions of the feeding of the five thousand and of the last supper came to the minds of the disciples. This breakfast seems to have a Eucharistic quality about it.

Consider:

9. Why do you think that "none of the disciples dared to ask [Jesus], 'Who are you?'" How does the statement, "They knew it was the Lord" fit with not daring to ask? How might Jesus' physical body have changed?

10. Though Jesus had commissioned the disciples (20:21), they returned for a night to their old trade, fishing. What might have motivated such a decision now that Jesus' physical presence was gone? What special motivation might Peter have had to dress and jump into the sea after Jesus was sighted?

The Resurrection and Beyond

John 21:15-23

Three times Jesus asks Peter if he loves Jesus. Three times Peter answers affirmatively. All four gospels record Peter's threefold denial of Christ. Jesus here gives Peter one opportunity for each denial to profess his love for his Lord. Peter is told, in response to his repeated protestations of love, to feed and tend the sheep. Jesus had been the shepherd to this point; now the responsibility for shepherding God's flock was handed over to Peter (and by extension, to the whole Church). Still, however, Peter could only be a shepherd as long as he, like a sheep, obeyed the call of Jesus the shepherd: "Follow me" (21:19).

Verses 18 and 19 are simply a prophecy that Peter was not going to die of natural causes, but as a martyr. These verses are not intended to give details of the manner of his death. By the time John wrote, Peter had probably already been executed.

Peter asks Jesus what John's fate is to be (21:21), and Jesus responds with a statement that evidently came to be widely misunderstood as a promise that John would not die. This misunderstanding was probably also encouraged by the fact that John lived to be quite old. John himself here takes pains to correct the misunderstanding (21:23). He himself has no notion that he will live forever on earth, but he believes in Jesus Christ and thus has a claim on eternal life.

11. If you denied knowing Jesus and then you were asked by him about the quality of your love for him, how would you feel? What might be your response? How would you know that you were forgiven? How does Jesus demonstrate his love for Peter in this passage? What seems to be most important to Jesus in this passage?

12. How could Peter be both a shepherd and a sheep at the same time? How can we? What does it mean for us in today's world to feed and tend Jesus' sheep? Give examples. What might be a contemporary analogy for the shepherd/sheep relationship?

13. Peter is curious about another's fate. How is Jesus' response (21:22) applicable to our relationships today?

John 21:24-25

"This is the disciple who is testifying to these things." That is, this other disciple, whom Jesus loved, is the author of this gospel. This assures the readers that the writer is an eyewitness to the events to which he testifies. This statement also certifies that this gospel belongs in the collection of sacred writing we call the New Testament, for at the time that the definitive list of New Testament books was developed, the primary qualification for inclusion was apostolic authorship.

The final verse in this gospel echoes the other concluding remarks found at the end of chapter 20, but adds one more thought: Whatever the reader has grasped of Jesus Christ from this gospel is not the whole. Human categories and methods of collecting history (as in books) are all insufficient to contain the full reality of Jesus Christ, just as these categories and methods cannot contain God. The Father and the Son share the characteristic of transcending our world. But the joy of the gospel is that the Father chose to be available to us through the gift of the Son to our world. Joy indeed!

Consider:

14. John insists that his witness is true—he has neither lied, nor exaggerated, nor distorted any of these events. When else are we dependent on another's testimony? Do you accept this book as the accurate record of an eyewitness? Why or why not?

Group Activities

1. Invite group members to arrive at a group definition of the terms below. Record these definitions on a chalkboard or on newsprint:

reconciliation	absolution
penitence	forgiveness
confession	contrition

2. Invite group members to read the original creation story in GENESIS 2:4-25. Ask them to brainstorm the following question:

   - In what ways are we new creations in Jesus Christ? How are we the same? How are we different?

   Record group members' ideas on chalkboard or newsprint.

3. Ask for two volunteers to roleplay Jesus' conversation with Peter (21:15-19). Instruct the volunteers to translate the whole discussion into modern speech, saying plainly what Jesus seems to be saying symbolically.

   When the roleplay is over, encourage other group members to offer their reactions to what was said by the two volunteers.

4. Mary only recognized Jesus when he said her name. Distribute an index card and a pen or pencil to each group member. Invite group members to respond on their index cards to the following questions:

   - If Jesus were to stand behind you today and speak your name, how would it sound? What would be its tone? What feelings would it produce in you? Why?

   Invite volunteers to share their thoughts with the group.

Journal Meditation

Close your eyes and imagine that you are sitting on the shore of the Sea of Tiberias at dawn, beside a small charcoal fire with Jesus and the disciples who have just spent the night fishing. What do you see? What do you smell? What do you hear? What do you feel under your feet? What does your clothing feel like? What is the temperature? Is there a breeze? What emotions are you experiencing as Jesus offers you bread and fish?

In the space below, draw the position of your hands (upturned, closed loosely, closed in a fist, hanging at your side, folded in your lap, etc.) as Jesus offers this breakfast. If this hand position does not seem satisfactory to you, indicate in a sentence or two what you would like to say to Jesus or have Jesus say to you to enable you to change the way you are holding your hands.

Stepstone to Prayer

Lord, you want to know if I love you. You know all things; you know that I...

Bibliography

Abbott-Smith, G. *A Manual Greek Lexicon of the New Testament*. Edinburgh: T. & T. Clark, 1937.

Barclay, William. *The Gospel of John*. Vols. 1 and 2, rev. ed. Philadelphia: The Westminster Press, 1975.

The Dictionary of Bible and Religion. William H. Gentz, ed. Nashville: Abingdon, 1986.

Harvey, A. E. *The New English Bible Companion to the New Testament*. Oxford University Press, Cambridge University Press, 1970.

Howard, W.F. *Christianity According to St. John*. London: Duckworth, 1943.

The Interpreter's Bible. Vol. 8. Nashville: Abingdon, 1952.

The Interpreter's One-Volume Commentary on the Bible. Charles M. Laymon, ed. Nashville: Abingdon, 1971.

Juel, Donald, et. al. *An Introduction to New Testament Literature*. Nashville: Abingdon, 1978.

Kittel, Gerhard and Gerhard Friedrich, eds. *Theological Dictionary of the New Testament*. abridged by Geoffrey W. Bromiley. Grand Rapids, Mich.: William B. Eerdmans Publishing Co., 1985.

The Life and Works of Josephus. William Whiston, trans. Philadelphia: The John C. Winston Co., n.d..

Morris, Leon. *The Gospel According to John*. Grand Rapids, Mich.: Wm. B. Eerdmans Publishing Co., 1971.

Neil, William. *Harper's Bible Commentary*. New York: Harper and Row, 1962.

The New International Version Study Bible. Grand Rapids, Mich.: Zondervan Bible Publishers, 1985.

Sanford, John A. *The Kingdom Within*. rev. ed. San Francisco: Harper and Row, 1987.

Sprague, Minka Shura. *One to Watch, One to Pray: A Devotional Introduction to the Gospels*. Wilton, Conn.: Morehouse-Barlow, 1985.